"In this classic work entitled *Christ*, Adolphe Monod (1802–1856) masterfully paints a portrait of Paul with a Scripture brush, showing us the apostle in the richness and fullness of his person. In this book, Monod shows himself to be a profound Pauline scholar of the highest order, setting forth the life of the great apostle as a worthy example for us to learn from and follow. This insightful and challenging volume is a must read for every lover of the apostle Paul, but more importantly, every lover of Christ, whom Paul sought to imitate so closely."

—ROB VENTURA
Pastor, Grace Community Baptist Church, North Providence, RI
Co-author of "A Portrait of Paul"

"The Christian Church in the West is in desperate need of revival. No argument there. Yet what shall we do to seek the life of Christ and allow it to reanimate our lives? Why not go back to St. Paul, whose theology became his biography? Why not return to the soul-stirring preaching of one man—a man called out by the risen Christ Himself—to guide us back to robust preaching, to fearless ministry, and to expectations that God will bless His Word, anoint our lips, save souls, transform lives, and establish His Kingdom? This new translation of the classic *Saint Paul* by Adolphe Monod, a godly 19th century French divine who was powerfully influenced by Erskine of Scotland, is exactly what we need to be reading. You will find that the nutrients of the Gospel in Monod's work on the Apostle provide instant relief from the current, Old Christendom, feckless theological contaminants. This is powerful stuff. It is the power unto salvation. My thanks to Solid Ground for lifting this up. We need it now more than ever."

—MICHAEL A. MILTON
Chancellor/CEO and
James M. Baird Jr. Professor of Pastoral Theology,
Reformed Theological Seminary

"Imagine the world if the Apostle Paul had not existed. Adolphe Monod, the spearhead of the French Réveil, asks and answers this question with pertinence. The world would be incomparably poorer. Though writing in the nineteenth century, he has brought the Apostle Paul to life for our own times, and indeed for all the ages. Contrary to popular images of Paul, this chief of the Apostles was a deeply feeling person, yet also a messenger of the Gospel whose God-given courage helped lay the foundation for the church as we know it. Once again, Constance K. Walker has faithfully translated this text in a way that loses nothing of the vividness of the original. This gem of a book is historically fascinating, theologically balanced, and a compelling inspiration for us to draw closer to the God of the Apostle Paul."

—WILLIAM EDGAR
Professor of Apologetics,
Westminster Seminary, Philadelphia PA

"Read this book! You will grow in Christ in new and different ways. You will see vividly what God's calling to you looks like. Monod was "the Voice of the [19th century French] Awakening," and as you read you'll know why. He asks the simple but arresting question: What was it that made Paul who he was? Why was he able to accomplish so much, so deeply? Are you thinking, it must have been just the right time for the gospel? Or, he must have had an amazing gift-package? Well, you're wrong, both times. It was a terrible time for the gospel, and Paul was weak in so many ways. He said that, over and over—yet we struggle to accept it. But this book will do it for you. Then, you can look at your own calling, but not by looking at your gifts. You'll learn how the Lord delights to use you in your humanity, as he did Paul, weaknesses and all."

—D. CLAIR DAVIS
Professor of Church History and Chaplain
Redeemer Seminary, Dallas TX

"Sustained study of the life and ministry of the Apostle Paul over the past thirty years has convinced me that his work was utterly essential to the foundation of the church in the apostolic era. And it is tremendous to have this classic study of Paul by Adolphe Monod, the great French preacher of the nineteenth century, lay out for us the importance of Paul's teaching and life. I am thrilled to recommend this old classic, newly translated into English."

—MICHAEL A. G. HAYKIN
Professor of Church History and Biblical Spirituality
The Southern Baptist Theological Seminary, Louisville KY
Director, The Andrew Fuller Center for Baptist Studies

SAINT

Paul

OTHER TITLES BY ADOLPHE MONOD

Living in the Hope of Glory

"Monod's dying testimony is instructing, enriching, inspiring."
—RICK PHILLIPS

An Undivided Love

"With unequaled passion and clarity he brings the unassuming listener not merely to the foot of the cross, but to Jesus himself."
—WILLIAM EDGAR

Jesus Tempted in the Wilderness

"A masterpiece, bringing together profound comfort, realistic understanding, practical wisdom, and heavenly glory."
—JOEL BEEKE

Woman, Her Mission and Her Life

"You will . . . wonder how any man could be so astute, so tender, so frank, and so inspiring in speaking to his Christian sisters"
—REBECCA CLOWNEY JONES

SAINT

Paul

CHANGING OUR WORLD
FOR CHRIST

ADOLPHE MONOD

CONSTANCE K. WALKER
EDITOR AND TRANSLATOR

SOLID GROUND
CHRISTIAN BOOKS
P.O. BOX 660132 • VESTAVIA HILLS • ALABAMA 35266

Cover image by Ken Jenkins
[For other examples of his work, please visit www.kenjenkins.com.]

Cover design by Constance K. Walker and Borgo Design

Printed in the United States of America

978-159925-2810

Adolphe Monod, 1802–1856

Contents

Biographical Sketch ✼

Adolphe Monod (1802–1856) has rightly been called "The Voice of the Awakening." Those who came out of curiosity to hear the preaching of a celebrated orator would often leave the service pierced to the heart by his message, while the mature Christians in his congregations came back again and again to be transported by his preaching into the very presence of God and to have their faith stretched and challenged. Others, including Aldophe's older brother, Frédéric, were more influential as leaders of the Awakening that swept across France and Switzerland in the early 19th century, but none could expound the central core of its faith quite as clearly or persuasively or appealingly as Adolphe Monod.

Yet Monod's faith did not come without a struggle. He was descended from Protestant ministers and received a clear call to the ministry at age fourteen, but the faith he grew up with was more formal than vibrant. In 1820 he entered seminary in Geneva, where the varied theological viewpoints soon left him in a state of spiritual confusion. He was often drawn toward the teaching of the Awakening, especially as presented by a Scotsman, Thomas Erskine, but his reason could not accept all of its teachings. Still confused, he accepted ordination in 1824.

Confusion turned to crisis when he agreed to pastor a group of French-speaking Protestants in Naples. He knew he could not express his doubts to the congregation, but his natural candor recoiled at preaching something he did not yet believe. Family members prayed earnestly for him, and once again he received help through a visit by Thomas Erskine.

Eventually, on July 21, 1827, he reached a state of peace. "I wanted to make my own religion, instead of taking it from God. . . . I was without God and burdened with my own well-being, while now I have a God who carries the burden for me. That is enough." He still had questions, but he knew he would find the answers in the pages of the Bible.

Shortly thereafter he was called to join the pastoral staff of the large but worldly Reformed Church in Lyon, where his bold, gospel-centered preaching soon drew opposition. He was told not to preach salvation by grace; he refused. They demanded his resignation; he refused. After much unpleasantness, the elders secured the government's permission to dismiss him, but a group of evangelical Christians who had already left the national church asked him to establish an independent congregation in Lyon. He served there until an unexpected call led him to the national church's seminary in Montauban. A decade later, in 1847, he returned to the pastorate, serving the Reformed Church in Paris. Quite ill and diagnosed with terminal cancer in 1855, he began holding small communion services in his home. These continued until his death on April 6, 1856, with his children writing down the brief meditations he gave.

Those facts, however, fail to truly capture the spirit of the man. His was a strong and passionate faith, in part because of his early spiritual struggles. He was also a man of great integrity, a keen mind, and a deeply caring, pastoral heart. All of these qualities were augmented and set off by his natural gift for speaking. Yet even as his renown grew, Adolphe Monod remained a truly humble man. A week before his death he said, "I have a Savior! He has freely saved me through his shed blood, and I want it to be known that I lean uniquely on that poured-out blood. All my righteous acts, all my works which have been praised, all my preaching that has been appreciated and sought after—all that is in my eyes only filthy rags."

TRANSLATOR'S PREFACE ✳

In *Saint Paul*, we discern the heart and soul behind much of Adolphe Monod's ministry. Yes, he wanted to lead his listeners and especially his parishioners to the foot of the cross so that they would commit their lives to Christ, but that was just the beginning. He also wanted to help raise up a generation of young people who would, through their faith and action, bring renewal to the church. Yet his ultimate goal was to see the renewed church transform society and change the world. That was the need in nineteenth century France, and it is still the need today.

If you want to find the energy and passion in the Christian church in the twenty-first century, the best place to look is not in the United States, or Great Britain, and certainly not in Western Europe. To be sure, there are strong Christians in each of these places, but the churches are, on the whole, comfortable and content. You can largely forget the "Christian" West. No, you would do better to look in places like Afghanistan, China, Myanmar, Iran—places where proclaiming faith in Christ can get you arrested, tortured, and even killed, places where it costs something to be a Christian. We in the West don't even want to be mocked or shunned by those around us. Yet if the church is to grow, if it is to recapture the vitality that makes it attractive, if it is to have a serious impact on society and culture, then we, its members, need to recapture the energy and passion that characterized the apostle Paul's ministry and that characterizes the persecuted church today. Adolphe Monod's goal in this series of discourses is to help us do that.

But beware! This is not a comfortable book. It is a serious, challenging, even radical book. In framing his arguments, the author chose, in a sense, to work backward. He starts from what we know about Saint Paul—the great work he accomplished in building the Gentile church and changing his world for Christ. At times this chapter might seem to belabor the obvious, but the intent is to encourage (and perhaps shame?) us with what God can do through someone who gives him a fully yielded heart. Then Monod asks how all of this work was possible. He considers first the nature of Paul's faith, then how God formed that faith through Paul's conversion, and lastly the natural gifts and weaknesses God placed in Paul before his conversion. The final discourse is a stark challenge to each of us who long to lead Christian lives that impact the world around us. It is especially an appeal to the young in our midst, who still have time and energy for such a great work. The point is not that we will do what Paul did; we won't. But we need to bring his spirit to the tasks God has appointed for us.

Ken Jenkins' cover image, "Morning Reflections," shows both the height and depth of the gospel Paul spent his life proclaiming, the gospel we are to live out. The height, represented by the mountains, is the gospel's ability to relate us to God and to the heavenly, eternal realm where he dwells. This upward dimension is reflected in our lives, represented by the lake, where it penetrates down to the very depths of our being and transforms us into new creatures in Christ.

As with my earlier translations of Monod's works, I have sought to preserve the author's style and "voice," while still allowing the text to flow naturally for a modern reader. Footnotes followed by Monod's initials in brackets, [A.M.], are his; all others were supplied for this translation. The text I worked from is the last volume of a four-volume set of Monod's sermons, published in Paris in 1860.

The translation and editing of Adolphe Monod's writings is a great privilege, but one in which I am keenly aware of my need for help, both divine and human. I am deeply grateful to writer Sarah G. Byrd for her insightful comments and suggestions; to Gwillim Law, grammar expert and master of detail, for his careful reading of the manuscript; to William Edgar who has once again served as my cultural and linguistic consultant; and to Ken Jenkins, whose magnificent cover image provides the "clothing" to adorn Monod's words and bring out their character. The labor of these faithful friends has produced a higher quality volume than I could otherwise have achieved. I also want to thank Michael Gaydosh at Solid Ground Christian Books for his continued enthusiasm for Monod's material and his commitment to making it available again today.

My prayer is that God, who guided Adolphe Monod in preparing these messages, might also have guided this translation and that he would deign to use it to accomplish his good purposes in a new generation of readers.

Constance K. Walker
Durham, North Carolina

RISE UP, O MEN OF GOD

Rise up, O men of God!
Have done with lesser things.
Give heart and mind and soul and strength
To serve the King of kings.

Rise up, O men of God!
The kingdom tarries long.
Bring in the day of brotherhood
And end the night of wrong.

Rise up, O men of God!
The church for you doth wait,
Her strength unequal to her task;
Rise up and make her great!

Lift high the cross of Christ!
Tread where His feet have trod.
As brothers of the Son of Man,
Rise up, O men of God!

William P. Merrill
(1867–1954)

SAINT PAUL

MONOD'S PREFACE

In these discourses, one need not look for a historical study of the life and writings of the apostle. The objective is humbler, more practical, and timelier. Jealous as I am to see the formation of a people of God able to respond to the spiritual task of the age, I am seeking a real and living example for them, and I find this example in Saint Paul.

I would like first to assess the good that Saint Paul did for the church and, through her, for the world. Then I want to study the moral driving force behind his immense activity, and finally, in this easily understood way, to propose him as an example.

I am speaking for those of my brothers in Jesus Christ who, have "decided to know nothing . . . except Jesus Christ and him crucified" (1 Corinthians 2:2). I am speaking for those who deplore with me the apathy of the faithful church and who, like me, are pursuing her reformation—called for from every side—through the growth of her spiritual life. These brothers, who are groaning but groaning in hope, wherever they may be and whatever name they may bear, have my full sympathy. Can I not also count on their love and their prayers?

I sense a greater than usual need of them. In these troubled and serious days, how does one speak, much less write, about the "one thing . . . needful" without holy fear and trembling? I know this fear and trembling all too well, and I beg my kind readers to accept nothing from me without subjecting it to the rule of Scripture: "Test everything; hold fast what is good" (1 Thessalonians 5:21).

———————

To return to Saint Paul, I want to express here a longing, deeply engraved in my heart: that our religious literature might be enriched by a history of the great apostle. Is there not some young minister of the gospel who will accomplish what was only a dream for me on entering my theological career? Is there not someone who will, from the start, take Saint Paul as the preferred object of his study and end up giving the church a deep work on his life and writings? He would find the way already opened by a number of publications, old and modern, French and foreign. To mention only our era, Neander[1] and the Germans would supply abundant and precious material.

———————

It will be noted that I sometimes stray from our usual versions in citing the Bible, even though the differences rarely affect the meaning of the text. Though I am jealous to see the original simplicity and force of sacred language restored—to the extent that our idiom allows it—I would, in general, have qualms about touching a text that has been consecrated by long usage and is held in general respect, except in the case of urgent necessity. As, however, there is work today on various sides to correct the French version, it seems to me that each ought to seize the opportunity to bring at least his small stone to the building of the new edifice. In

———————

[1] Neander has summed up his own views on Saint Paul in a popular form through two articles in the excellent collection published by Dr. Piper of Berlin, from which I here borrow more than once. (*Evangelisches Jahrbuch, 1850: Pauli Bekehrung; Pauli Leben und Leiden.*) [A.M.]

the present work, I often make use of the New Testament that appeared in 1839 in Lausanne under the title, *The New Testament of our Lord Jesus Christ, translated from the original by a group of ministers of the Word of God.* This version, too literal, in my view, to be adopted for common worship, offers a precious advantage stemming from this very fault. Scrupulously exact, it stands in place of the original, as much as that is feasible, for those who have no recourse to it. This large class of readers of the New Testament should always have the Lausanne version at hand, at least in order to consult it.

HIS PRODIGIOUS WORK

HIS PRODIGIOUS WORK

1 Corinthians 15:10

I worked harder than any of them.

THE NEED OF THE HOUR

My brothers,

To renew Christian society through a restored Christian church—this is the objective the true disciple of Jesus Christ, and more especially the true minister of Jesus Christ, sets for himself today.[1] Everything proclaims and everyone foresees that the time is drawing near when the Christian church will be returned to this great mission, so forgotten in the disorder and crisis of the present situation. The time is drawing near,

---

[1] Here, by "Christian society" Monod would seem to be referring to the society around him in France specifically and Western Europe more generally. Historically Christian, they had strayed from their biblical moorings, particularly with the many turbulent political crises in France that occurred during Monod's lifetime.

but has it arrived? I have difficulty convincing myself that it has. If it had arrived, men of good will would not be so divided on how to reconstitute the church on foundations of sufficient strength and breadth.[2]

A HEALTHY CHURCH; A SANCTIFIED PEOPLE

But while waiting for this time to arrive, we need to hasten it through an analogous though different work, a spiritual work that must precede the ecclesiastical work. I have spoken to you about it more than once, and, if it pleases God, I will speak about it more than once again, because it is one of the major concerns of my ministry.

"A people for Jesus Christ's own possession" (see Titus 2:14) needs to be formed, gathered from all of the Christian communions in the name of that which is most vital to the Christian faith and life. They are to walk in the love of Christ and in the footsteps of Christ through the grace of Christ. They are to go "about doing good" (Acts 10:38) and rehabilitate the gospel—so compromised in men's minds—by visibly displaying both what it is and what it can do.

A ROLE-MODEL

The formation of this life-giving people requires an example on which it can be modeled; the mere depiction of

---

[2] In 1848, three years before these discourses were first published, a revolution in France ushered in the Second Republic and a fresh period of political uncertainty that impacted every area of society, including the church. The Reformed Church of France, of which Adolphe Monod was a minister, was under a strong measure of government control and passed through a very painful crisis. A number of evangelical Christians, including Adolphe Monod's eldest brother, left the "national" church to form a new, independent denomination, while Adolphe chose to remain and work for reform.

the Christian life in the gospel is not enough. The distance separating desiring from doing, both in us and around us, is so great that the most firmly established theory only inspires a certain involuntary defiance in us unless practice comes to its aid. The more gospel morality is holy in our eyes, the more we need to see it exemplified in a living man—or at least in a man who has lived—in order for it to appear possible.

But do we not have this desired example in "the man Christ Jesus" (1 Timothy 2:5), that living law in whom the ideal merges with the real? Undoubtedly, and you all know that his example, the only perfect example, is also the one to which I appeal in all my discourses. Yet the very perfection of this model, while giving it unique value, also invites us to seek something else, not quite so elevated above our reach and thus more accessible to our imitation and more humiliating for our unfaithfulness.

Very well, I have come to offer you this second-order type—someone eminent without being perfect—in the person of an apostle who, through his faithfulness in following the Master's example, has gained the right to propose himself as an example. "Be imitators of me, as I am of Christ" (1 Corinthians 11:1).

WHY PAUL?

Saint Paul is not the only model in gospel history I could have chosen, but he is, to my mind, the most complete. In addition, setting aside the question of personal superiority, I have two other reasons for preferring him. Of all the apostles, Saint Paul is the one whose story is best known to us and the one who interests us most directly, having been established by God as the apostle to the Gentiles and thus to us, the offspring of those Gentiles.

Moreover, do not fear any tributes from me in which the saint of the day usurps the place reserved for his Master and ours. Beyond the fact that the imperfection of the scene is as necessary to me as its beauty in the program I am proposing, it would not be true to Saint Paul's spirit to give him something that only belongs to the Lord. If I were to forget myself to that extent, I would expect to see his image throw itself in front of me and cry out to me, as he once did to the residents of Lystra, "Men, why are you doing these things? We also are men, of like nature with you" (Acts 14:15).

All the grace I ask of God is to be true, knowing well that there is in our apostle enough holiness to place him well above us along with enough weakness to keep him well below "the Lord of glory" (1 Corinthians 2:8, James 2:1).

PAUL AND THE CHRISTIAN REVOLUTION

If someone asked me who among all men appears to me to be the greatest benefactor of our species, without hesitation I would name the apostle Paul. For me, his name represents the most extensive and, at the same time, most useful example of human activity that history has preserved for us.

THE CHRISTIAN REVOLUTION

No one, believer or not, will argue that the revolution brought about by Jesus Christ is the greatest and most beneficial that has ever been accomplished in the world. As proof I have a witness even more reliable than that of historians: the witness of all civilized peoples. They have so keenly sensed that Jesus Christ is the key to the vault of humanity and the center of its whole history, that they have numbered their years beginning with him.

We are in the year 1851, but why? Because there are one thousand, eight hundred and fifty one years since Jesus Christ came. Beyond that, we calculate the same way even for the times that preceded his coming, in spite of the awkwardness of counting backwards. Before or after, the place that an event or a man has in history is marked by the distance that separates it from Jesus Christ. So let's not make a game of substantiating the evidence; the establishment of Christianity in the world is the event of events.

The Author of this revolution was more than a man, yet he employed simple men, the apostles, as his instruments. Under him, they became the agents of the most extensive and most fruitful movement that has ever stirred mankind. The spiritual seed they sowed from place to place in the bosom of our poor earth has changed its face. The freeing of slaves, the emancipation of women, the elevation of domestic life, the improvement of laws, the softening of manners, the diffusion of knowledge, the progress (I should have said the creation) of benevolence, perhaps even the world reborn to new life—such is the fruit that we gather each day from their labor. Yet, ungrateful as we are, we fail to remember the faithful hands through which God sowed this fruit for our benefit.

The Role of the apostles

There is an apostle and then there is an apostle. Jesus Christ had twelve apostles, augmented by a thirteenth with Paul's conversion, and he divided among them the two great tasks involved in the world's regeneration: the evangelization of the Jews and that of the Gentiles.

The Jews were but a single nation, small and despised; the Gentiles occupied the rest of the globe and numbered in their ranks the most glorious peoples on earth. Is it not true that you would have kept the greater number of apostles for the greater of the two works? But God's ways are not our ways. Except for the inevitable interpenetration of these two works and for the beginnings of both promised to Simon Peter, God leaves the twelve apostles to the Jews and gives the Gentiles only one, whom he forms expressly for them. He will be called the apostle to the Gentiles, or simply the Apostle, because just this name was a clear enough designation among the children of the Gentiles.[3]

Corresponding to the special calling that made Paul an apostle set apart, there was in him a kind of jealous attention given to disengaging his mission from that of others.[4] A spiritual Atlas, Paul, by himself, bore the pagan world on his shoulders.

PAUL'S SPECIAL TASK

The Roman Empire, which an entire people (and the most powerful people on earth) took seven centuries to form, was renewed by this one single man in a quarter of a century. That is his work, his special work. I was going to say his exclusive work, because the work of Saint Peter in Caesarea and Antioch, of Saint John in Ephesus and Patmos, not to mention the work of the second tier of apostles—Barnabas, Timothy, Titus, and so many others—all pale beside Paul's!

In comparing himself with all the other apostles put together, Paul has gained the right to say, in a spirit of humility and with thanksgiving, "By the grace of God I am what I am, and his grace toward me was not in vain. On the contrary, I worked harder than any of them, though it was not I, but the grace of God that is with me" (1 Corinthians

---

[3] See Galatians 2:7–8 with regard to this division. [A.M.]
[4] See Romans 15:20–21, etc. [A.M.]

15:10). Jesus Christ made the apostles the greatest of men, and the greatest of the apostles is Saint Paul.

But let us leave this relative evaluation aside and take our apostle's labor by itself. Let us, if we can, gain an awareness of the good Saint Paul has done for the world.

THE EXTENT OF PAUL'S LABORS

Do not think, however, that I intend for us to follow our apostle through all the work he carried out during the roughly thirty years of his apostleship.[5] Think what that would involve!

We would have to follow him traveling as he did throughout the world at a time when such travels were slow, difficult, and dangerous.

We would have to follow him preceding his missionary life with four or five years spent in the isolation of Arabia, in the evangelization of Damascus, in the flight from Damascus to Jerusalem and from Jerusalem to Tarsus, and in his direction of the new people of Antioch, where the new name of Christian was introduced.

We would have to follow him as he traversed the vast Roman Empire, directed by the voice of the Holy Spirit who called him. He seemingly skimmed the ground, to judge only by the breadth of his travels; yet he dug deeply, if we believe the trail he left behind him as he sowed the earth in passing with a string of nascent churches stretching from Jerusalem to Rome (if not beyond) and from Rome to Jerusalem.

We would have to follow him on his first missionary journey, as he crossed the isle of Cyprus from Salamis to Paphos, converting the proconsul and stopping the mouth

---

[5] The most reliable chronology places Paul's conversion between the years 30 and 40 and his death between the years 60 and 70. (Neander, etc.) [A.M.]

of the false prophet. From there he ran on into Pisidia—to
the cities of Antioch, Iconium, Lystra, Derbe, Perga, and
Attalia—going from the Jews to the Gentiles and often
rejected by both. He was, in turn, both worshipped as a god
by a delirious people and stoned in fury by the same people.
Nonetheless he went back through all the churches to provide them with pastors.

We would have to follow him on his second missionary
journey, as he took up his travels again following new labors
in Antioch and Jerusalem. This time he crossed the straits
and filled Europe with the name of the unknown God,
founding the churches of Philippi, Thessalonica, Berea,
Athens, Corinth, and others I could name.

We would have to follow him on his third missionary
journey, embracing both Europe and Asia in his immense
inspection tour. Reckoning by province, he visited Galatia,
Phrygia, and Ephesus—that is to say, all the western part of
Asia Minor—plus Macedonia and Greece. Then, on the way
back, he visited Troas (with the resurrection of one who
was dead), Miletus (with his inimitable farewell discourse),
Cyprus, Tyre, Ptolemais, Caesarea, and finally Jerusalem.
There the rage of the Jews and the chains of the Romans
awaited him.

We would have to follow him on his fourth missionary
journey as an apostle-prisoner but prisoner-apostle. He was
carried through storms on a ship that would not have been
lost if only it had listened to him, and he dispensed present
life along with eternal life to his companions in danger. As a
poor castaway, he repaid the hospitality of Malta with the
creation of a church and arrived finally in Rome only to bring
the gospel right into Caesar's household.

We would have to follow him where the book of Acts no
longer does and where we are left with a few scattered bits of
information from his last epistles. We would have to follow
him in these last journeys right up to his second captivity

in Rome and to those words filled with his impending martyrdom, "For I am already being poured out as a drink offering, and the time of my departure has come" (2 Timothy 4:6).

Even if I had the time, even if I had the courage, following him in this way would not do justice to my subject. For how can one communicate in human speech all the activity and action in that life whose hero wearies the historian? How can one communicate the battles, the joys, the sorrows, the prayers, and the deep inner travail, without which the outward travail would offer us only a body deprived of a soul?

PAUL'S OWN ASSESSMENT

Word for word, I would much prefer to cite the apostle himself and to join him in summing up his external labor in the simple testimony he gave in writing to the Romans when he was still only halfway through his course. "For I will not venture to speak of anything except what Christ has accomplished through me to bring the Gentiles to obedience—by word and deed, by the power of signs and wonders, by the power of the Spirit of God—so that from Jerusalem and all the way around to Illyricum, I have fulfilled the ministry of the gospel of Christ" (Romans 15:18–19).

Similarly, I would join him in summing up his internal labors in the appeal he addressed to the consciences of the Corinthians after concisely enumerating all that he had suffered for the name of the Lord. "And apart from other things, there is the daily pressure on me of my anxiety for all the churches. Who is weak, and I am not weak? Who is made to fall, and I am not indignant?" (2 Corinthians 11:28–29).

Saint Paul's missionary life is one of those tableaux too grandiose for any attempt to depict them "full face"; one must take them in profile. Therefore, let us be content with appreciating his work indirectly, and let us measure it by its results.

THE RESULTS OF PAUL'S VOYAGES

I hold before me a map of the Roman Empire. There I see famous cities, centers of power and civilization, in the East and in the West: Antioch, Tarsus, Ephesus, Thessalonica, Athens, Corinth, Rome, and so many others. Then I ask myself, "In these cities and in the regions they represent, what was the moral and religious state of the population before Paul's mission began, and what was their state when it was ended by his martyrdom?" To make the question more precise, let us limit it to just one of these cities. Ephesus will serve as an example for all.

EPHESUS BEFORE PAUL'S ARRIVAL

A blind and childish superstition had invaded Ephesus, placed as it was under the protection of a false divinity, the fierce and vindictive Diana. Her temple was celebrated throughout the world for the magnificence of its architecture, the richness of its adornments, and the beauty of its statues. All the different kinds of idolatry—idolatry of images, of gold, of antique art—were gathered together in her bosom, as if to ensure the seduction of every mind. A moral corruption unknown even in our corrupt generation had followed after this erroneous doctrine, in which it found both its justification and its sustenance.

Only a few superior men escaped this universal impulse, yet for the most part, having exhausted the full resources of their genius and study, they were left to throw themselves into a desolate and desperate skepticism, which is the fatal end of all the wisdom of the wise. Or perhaps they reattached themselves to one or the other of the two philosophical systems that prided themselves on responding to the elevated needs of human nature. One, stoicism, intoxicated them through pride of mind and an ungodly deification of themselves; the other, Platonism, led them astray into a sentimental spiritualism which, far from directly attacking vulgar fanaticism, consecrated it in the guise of purifying it.

What then was left to the human spirit, devoid of light and faith, aspiring to the truth but mired in the material world? It could only call to its aid the folly of the magic arts—the illusory attempt to fill the chasm separating the visible world from the invisible—or perhaps that immoral pact with the spirit of darkness against the Spirit of God.

Add to all of that the fact that one portion of the city was enslaved to the other, that the poor were crushed more than has been seen anywhere in modern times, that women were abased along with all of domestic life, and that debauchery had become a byword.[6]

Then imagine, if you can, the frightful confusion that such a state of things would engender in one's mind and conduct. There would be nothing before him but a world heading off into dissolution, with no knowledge of how to stop the working of its moral disintegration. Meanwhile, the noble but vague aspirations of a few minds, a few hearts, perhaps a few select consciences would be lost, fading away like an empty sound in the air.

This is the humiliating and dismal picture that glorious Ephesus[7] (not to mention Antioch or Athens or Rome or the other capitals of the civilized world) presents to the eye of the impartial and careful observer, as long as the doctrine of

---

[6] See Romans 1:32. [A.M.]

[7] The word translated "glorious" can also have the meaning "prideful" or "arrogant."

Jesus Christ has not extended beyond the narrow confines of Judea.[8]

THE CHURCH'S EFFECT

Now let us move forward thirty years. Thirty years is not much time for a spiritual reform. The past thirty years in France will be counted in history among the generations that have most thoroughly shaken opinions and ideas. They have produced so many admirable inventions, so many surprising discoveries, so many remarkable new things. Yet what have we gained during these thirty years in the areas of religion and morality, which have no innovation to pursue but a return to the ancient teachings of the gospel? We have gained something, I recognize that. We have gained a more serious attention toward the things of God, yes. We have gained a small number of people called to the knowledge of Jesus Christ and glorifying him through a new life, yes again. But as to evidence of a deep and extensive reform, we have gained nothing.

Such was not the case in Ephesus during the thirty years—I could say the twenty years—that preceded the year 65 of our era.[9]

Here we are in Ephesus in the year 65. Barely five years still separate us from the day when the destruction of Israel's temple and nationality will finally deliver God's kingdom to the Gentiles. About twenty years ago, an event both very small and very great took place in our city. A Christian church was born, emerging from the midst of paganism like an island from the midst of the sea.

---

[8] Neander, *Histoire de la religion et de l'Église, durant les trois premiers siècles*, Introduction. [A.M.]

[9] The church in Ephesus was founded around the year 45, at the end of Saint Paul's second missionary journey (Acts 18). [A.M.]

This church is in no way exceptional, like her older sister in Jerusalem. She has not adopted, so far as we know, the holy sharing that characterized a charity almost too heavenly for this earth, yet she is a living church that displays the spirit of Jesus Christ and reveals it to the world through the measure of her faith and love. Neither does she number her new disciples by the thousands in a single day, yet she is large enough to call for the services of several pastors.[10] Besides, it is not numbers that determine influence here; it is faithfulness. Jesus Christ is only one, yet he fixes upon himself the attention first of an entire people, then of all the peoples of the earth. This is what every church, large or small, that inherits his spirit along with his name will do. Such is the church in Ephesus.

As evidence of the church's effect, I could cite the divine Word being carried from the synagogue into a school of philosophy and spreading from there throughout the surrounding region. I could cite the power of this word declared by the sinners who "came, confessing and divulging their practices" (Acts 19:18) and by their books on the magic arts that were burned in the public square and whose "value . . . came to fifty thousand pieces of silver" (Acts 19:19). Finally I could cite the silversmiths who made temples of Diana fearing the loss of their goddess' glory and their own trade (Acts19:24–40).

But let us set all of that aside and stop at the mere presence, the mere existence of a Christian church in Ephesus. The church is there before the eyes of the Ephesians. That is enough.

Henceforth, neither truth nor holiness can be passed off as an illusion; nor can superstition, unbelief, and intemperance be passed off as deplorable necessities of the human condition. Faced with the Christian church in Ephesus,

---

[10] See Acts 20:17, 37. [A.M.]

whoever sighs after what is good and true has found what will satisfy him. Faced with this same church, whoever still gives himself over to error and evil is convicted of lying and willful straying. There is an abundant resource open for the one[11] and a ready condemnation prepared for the other.[12] The only thing the witnesses of this moral phenomenon still need is the upright heart that Jesus Christ himself must find in a man in order to do his work in him.[13] The seed that will yield the precious fruit that the population of Ephesus is unknowingly seeking has come. It is there in the new church and needs only to grow.

Let it grow, and behold the life of the Spirit, the abundant life (John 10:10) that will replace the luxuriant but lost and wayward sap of a completely prodigal life of the flesh.

Let it grow, and behold a divine charity, an unknown brotherhood, a public and private benevolence unnamed in antiquity that will take the place of unbridled and shameless egotism.

Let it grow, and behold the dawn of an affection in the household between husband and wife, between parents and children, between master and servants that will turn the family into the cradle, the school, and the church of a regenerate people.

Let it grow, and that is enough for a new world to be raised up in Ephesus on the ruins of the former world. In this new world, on finding "the living and true God" (1 Thessalonians 1:9), man will also find himself.

THE EFFECT SPREADS

I have spoken only of Ephesus, but the same light has been lit in Antioch, Tarsus, Thessalonica, Athens, Corinth,

---

11 1 Corinthians 14:24–25. [A.M.]

12 Ephesians 5:11–13. [A.M.]

13 John 3:20–21, Luke 16:31, Mark 6:5–6. [A.M.]

Rome, and a multitude of other cities of lesser importance. Give these scattered centers time to communicate with one another, and the heavenly flame will gradually spread to cover the entire Roman Empire before it extends to the rest of the earth.

I seem to be giving prophesy while only giving history. Yes, the result has justified this happy prediction in exact proportion with the faithfulness of the church. Because the church bit by bit slackens in its faith and life, it only imperfectly carries out this great mission, but because it still has something of Jesus Christ, it carries out a certain measure of it.

Clearly, in spite of all that is lacking in our modern society, one would have to be truly blind, unfair, and ungrateful not to recognize its superiority over society at the time of Jesus Christ. Half of humanity was in servitude, women were ignored and debased, the sanctuary of the home was profaned through the worship of sin, materialism was accepted by the human spirit as its end and almost as its source of rest, gladiators were slaughtering one another for the amusement of the Roman ladies, and foreign kings were dragged in fetters behind the chariot of their triumphant conqueror. We do not have all those horrors.

Yes, during the generation that flowed from the year 35 to the year 65, the Roman Empire was sown with the seed of eternal life. This seed, originating in heaven but introduced into humanity, contained the kernel of a complete revolution—not just moral but domestic, civil, political, and even material—if the world were faithful to cultivate it.

PAUL THE SOWER

Very well, who sowed this healthy seed whose field is the pagan world? Go to Ephesus and ask who gave them a Christian Church. Ephesus will answer in unison, "the apostle Paul." Ask in Tarsus; "the apostle Paul." Ask in Thessalonica; "the apostle Paul." Ask in Athens; "the apostle Paul." Ask in Corinth; "the apostle Paul."

Does this enumeration weary you? Let's shorten things. Ask in Salamis, Paphos, Pisidian Antioch, Iconium, Lystra, Derbe, Perga, Troas, Philippi, Berea, and Cenchreae; ask in Galatia, Phrygia, Pamphylia, Cilicia, and so many others; "the apostle Paul."

And what about the two great capitals, Antioch and Rome, one of the Grecian east, the other of the Roman west? If they cannot tell you that the apostle Paul founded their churches, they will tell you that he so strengthened them through his words that they consider him to have done more toward founding them than the founders themselves. One he exhorted many times in the Lord; the other he visited twice after having nurtured it through the divine letter that Saint Chrysostom has called "the golden key to the Scriptures." [14]

Amazing what one man, one single man can do! The marvelous activity of our apostle lends him a sort of omnipresence throughout the Roman world, and Paul's name casts an immense shadow across its vast extent. What are we, the preachers or missionaries of today, before such a man? (For truly, we have to work at remembering that this is a man, a simple man.) Would his story not appear unbelievable to us if it were recounted elsewhere than in the divine Scriptures? Would we not say he was one of those fabled giants to whose adventures fact barely contributes a humble portion or a modest starting point?

What has become of those grand figures of the first century? Is their race forever extinct, the mold broken, the tradition lost? Are they like those vanished animals who reveal their time on our earth only through fragments of their dried bones?

---

[14] In addition, there is reason to believe that the church in Rome was founded by disciples of Saint Paul. [A.M.]

But no! The way Paul appears to our lax generation must be the way Moses or Samuel appeared to the more-than-lax generation in which Saul of Tarsus recognized the light. It is also very nearly the way Luther or Calvin still appear to us today. Prophets, apostles, reformers—those great men of God separated by so many centuries—were all found at the time God needed them, and they would be found again today if the faith of their hearts were reborn in one of their descendents. As Luther said in his admirable statement, "If I had the faith of Abraham, I would be Abraham."

PAUL'S ENDURING EFFECT

Whatever the case, whether or not such a prodigious career would be possible in other times, we see it supplied by Saint Paul. You could assess it no more accurately than in asking what would have changed in the history of the world if this one man had never been born.

If the world were lacking you or me, the effect would scarcely be felt outside the circle of a few friends, of a restricted public, or at most a generation or two. But lacking Saint Paul, who can calculate the enormous consequences in the sayings, the morals, the literature, the history, the whole development of the human race, beginning with our old Europe? Europe can fully apply to itself what Paul wrote to the Christians of Thessalonica: "For what is our hope or joy or crown of boasting before our Lord Jesus at his coming? Is it not you? For you are our glory and joy" (1 Thessalonians 2:19–20).

Lacking Saint Paul, watch out, stand aside, or fear lest you be buried beneath the ruins of the whole social edifice of eighteen centuries crumbling on its foundations.

Lacking Saint Paul, erase all the churches that were born by the hundreds in his footsteps; raise up again the temples and the idols he knocked down, not with his hands—that's not the apostolic way—but by the mere virtue of his word.

Lacking Saint Paul, remove the seeds that he planted from place to place, those fertile seeds of regeneration for the individual, the family, and society; plunge Europe and the Roman Empire back in the barbarism of a civilization "having no hope and without God" (Ephesians 2:12).

Yet truly, who am I talking about? Is it the Son of God? No, it is only his humble messenger. But this is a messenger animated by God's grace, a messenger who, with a sickly body and feeble speech, has shown us what one man, one simple man can do when he wants only what God wants.[15]

Nevertheless, let us agree that something is missing in this account of Saint Paul's labor. There is no point of comparison, no relationship to us and to our personal experience. We will draw closer to that in contemplating our apostle's labor through the work that still endures today and whose direct influence we feel every day. We will see it in his written word.

THE EFFECT OF PAUL'S WRITINGS

Saint Peter's precaution, "I will make every effort so that after my departure you may be able at any time to recall these things" (2 Peter 1:15), was likewise taken by Paul, and taken more broadly by him than by Saint Peter or any other apostle. Here again he has the right to say, "I worked harder than any of them" (1 Corinthians 15:10). Two-thirds of the apostolic letters bear the name of our apostle.

THE LABOR OF WRITING

Perhaps some will be astonished at the place I assign to Saint Paul's correspondence within his apostolic labors. Are

---

[15] John 15:7. [A.M.]

fourteen letters, of which the longest does not exceed sixteen chapters, such a great work? And however great it might be, should we not give credit to divine inspiration rather than to man's activity? Yet such surprise would be ill-considered, or else it would imply a rather narrow conception either of man's action or of God's.

A writer's labor is not measured by the number of pages he has written. A great tragic actor of modern times said somewhere (forgive me this comparison, but I need it to clarify my thinking for you), "People are grateful to me for awakening ideas in the minds of a crowd through a single phrase, something apparently quite simple. It seems as if my intonation were but the page of a book, whereas in reality it is the product of an entire book of reflections."

What makes this thought profound is its truth. Though borrowed from a kind of event that has justly fallen into discredit, it nevertheless sheds light on many things that go beyond the vulgar, because all human greatness touches at certain points. The intonation of a Roscius is like a stroke of Raphael's brush or a blow of Michelangelo's chisel. It takes only an instant to accomplish, but it takes years of preparation.

Let us speak only of the art of writing, the art most closely resembling the labor I am considering with our apostle. Each of the rich phrases that you admire in a great writer is the fruit of a long series of thoughts and experiences. Through a two-fold effort, he first had to gather them from every side and then distill them into a weighty summary. In reading it, you say, "It is only a line," but what you fail to see beneath this line is the infinite multitude of trials and deletions that went before it. I am not speaking of the trials and deletions that were made on paper, though it would be fair to consider those also. I am speaking of the trials and deletions that took place in the inner man—in the mind, in the heart, in the conscience. I am speaking of the trials and deletions that took place through meditation and reading, through watches and testings, through mourning, blood, and tears.

Now suppose that this great writer is a great apostle. He is more than a great philosopher, since his mind will draw from the depths of divine truth, and more than a poet, since his imagination will be reinvigorated on the heights of the divine spirit. An apostle is one of those clouds wandering between heaven and earth, charged with fire from on high and hurling its lightning bolts into the midst of earth's darkness, illuminating with sudden clarity a man's spiritual horizon—or rather that of all humanity.

Consider the statements, "I can do all things through [Christ] who strengthens me" (Philippians 4:13), or "When I am weak, then I am strong" (2 Corinthians 12:10), or again "For to me to live is Christ, and to die is gain" (Philippians 1:21). Who can doubt that each of these rays of light reveals a long, serious, painful labor in the mind and heart from which it emerged?

THE ROLE OF DIVINE INSPIRATION

Inspiration, especially of the New Testament, changes nothing. In inspiration, God's Spirit unites with man's spirit almost as the divine nature unites with human nature in the incarnation. If the Son of God present within Jesus Christ does not hinder the Son of man's painful participation in birthing salvation, neither does the divine word vibrating within the apostle's human word hinder the human word's laborious participation in announcing salvation. God and man in the first case, and the Spirit of God and the spirit of man in the second do not diminish one another; they are each complete, side by side with one another.

Moreover, each of the phrases I just cited (and that I chose almost at random from the first pages of our apostle that came to me), in spite of being found in the celestial regions of the divine Spirit, is no less to be sought in the intimate depths of the human spirit—in the lessons of experience, in the bitterness of hardship, in the formation and growth of the new man, and in the long apprenticeship of the spiritual life.

Who can say what battles had to be waged in the natural heart before conceiving—or, if you prefer, before receiving—the fourth chapter of Saint John's first epistle? The instruments of the Holy Spirit seem like the spoiled children of inspiration to the eyes of the ordinary person, yet they are its martyrs. Blessed be the fire that descends from heaven! But woe to the cloud charged with transmitting it to earth, whether he wearies himself in order to contain it or rends himself to give it free passage![16]

Thus I could, with good reason, speak of the prodigious labor implicit in letters such as those that come to us from the apostle Paul. Yet this thought would not strike all minds equally, so I mainly want to evaluate the apostle's writings, as I did his journeys, by the fruit they have borne and by the good they have done for the world.

THE FRUIT OF PAUL'S WRITINGS

What fruit have Saint Paul's writings borne? What good have they done for the world? To find out, you have no need to question either remote antiquity or unknown coastlands. Question yourselves and, based on your answer, judge for everyone else.

You have had no relationship with Saint Paul except through his writings, and yet you feel you have known him personally. There is so much life and warmth pulsating in his words that one could imagine merely stretching out a hand to

---

[16] See Jeremiah 20:8–9, Daniel 10:8, etc. [A.M.]

feel the beat of this heart that ceased beating nearly eighteen hundred years ago. Grateful reader of Saint Paul, are you not anticipating with holy impatience the day when, in "eternal dwellings" (Luke 16:9), you can tell the apostle "what God has done for your soul" (see Psalm 66:16) through his ministry? Then I appeal to you henceforth to bear witness to the part Saint Paul's epistles have played in your spiritual growth.

Do you recall the letter to the Romans? And have you read anywhere else, even in the Bible, such a complete, substantive, and persuasive exposition of the prophet's saying, "The righteous shall live by his faith" (Habakkuk 2:4)? Paul explains it as salvation given by God "freely by his grace" (Romans 3:24 KJV) through faith in Jesus Christ and communicating to the soul, one after the other, a life of righteousness (Romans 1–4), a life of peace (Romans 5), and a life of holiness (Romans 6–8).

Do you recall the letter to the Galatians? And have you read anywhere else, even in the Bible, a more concise, more lucid explanation of the secret relationships that unite the two covenants to one another, or a more solid demonstration of the superiority of the dispensation of the Spirit over that of the letter? The one suppresses the visible glory of the other only to bring out the invisible glory, which alone is real.

Do you recall the two letters to the Corinthians? And have you read anywhere else, even in the Bible, a more instructive and extensive collection of practical directions for the Christian life? It touches on church discipline, the celebration of the sacraments, the administration of God's gifts, woman's mission, and the exercise of benevolence.

And what about the letter to the Ephesians, giving instruction on the natural distinction and the spiritual fusion of the two peoples that make up Jesus Christ's new people? And what about the Pastoral Epistles, giving instruction for the ministry of pastors? What about the letter to Philemon, giving instruction for the spirit of Christian charity? . . .

I have not said everything, but how can everything be said?

OUR BIBLES WITHOUT PAUL

I asked a while ago what the world would lose if Saint Paul were lacking in the world. Now I ask what your soul would lose if Saint Paul were lacking in the Bible. Take out of your New Testament those hundred pages where you read Paul's name at the top. To be sure, I am not going so far as to say there isn't enough left in your Bible to save you. All we need for salvation is Jesus Christ, and it takes so very little for us to know Jesus Christ—just a word from his mouth, a word from one of his disciples, a word from the Old Testament. What am I saying? All it takes is a simple name, a name lisped in an obscure promise in the ear of the first man, long before anything was written and before there was any question of a Bible in the world.[17]

A little bread and water is enough to live on, yet we gather with thanksgiving the substantive nourishment God gives us in the flesh of animals, the exquisite fruit he hangs from the trees to refresh our parched palates, and the blood of the plentiful grapes he commands the vine to produce in order "to gladden the heart of man" (Psalm 104:15). Similarly, we could save our souls without Saint Paul in our Bible, true, but think what solid nourishment, what delicious re-

---

[17] This is a reference to John Calvin's statement in his Institutes of the Christian Religion, "Who is so devoid of intellect as not to understand that God, in so speaking, lisps with us as nurses are wont to do with little children? Such modes of expression . . . accommodate the knowledge of him to our feebleness. In so doing, he must of course, stoop far below his proper height." The verb for *lisp* commonly used in this quote in French (*bégayer*) is the same verb that Monod uses here.

freshment, what beneficial virtue we would be denied in losing those hundred pages!

Where would you have learned as much about the pathway—so new and yet so simple—of justification by faith without works, if Saint Paul had not written the first four chapters of his letter to the Romans?

Or about the inestimable, supreme, and unique value of love before God and men, if Saint Paul had not written the dear and precious thirteenth chapter of his first letter to the Corinthians?

Or about the glory of domestic life for the Christian—the place of Jesus Christ between husband and wife, between parents and children, between masters and servants—if Saint Paul had not written the fifth chapter of his letter to the Ephesians?

Or about the powerful value of each help God places at our disposal for holy warfare, if Saint Paul had not depicted the full armor of the soldier of Jesus Christ in the sixth chapter of the same epistle?

Or about the state to which a Christian's holiness is allowed to aspire, if Saint Paul had not written the last chapter of his first epistle to the Thessalonians?

Where would you have learned as much about the law holding us captive to sin without Romans 7? Or about the rejection of the Jews becoming the calling of the Gentiles without Romans 11? Or about the seed of true strength without 2 Corinthians 12? Or about the deep meaning of Moses without Galatians 4? Or about the relationship between faith and works without Ephesians 2? Or about all the rest without all the rest?

Ah, if you are not the most ungrateful of men or the most unbelieving, rise up and confess that among all mortals who have passed beneath the vault of heaven, there is none to whom you owe more, none to whom you owe as much as you owe to Saint Paul.

The World's Bibles Without Paul

So much for us, but broaden your gaze a bit further. Look to the right, to the left, ahead, and behind. See these hundred pages, translated into two hundred languages, drawing the same testimony not just from the English, the Germans, the Italians, the Spaniards, the Greeks, and the Russians, but also from the inhabitants of Asia, even to the depths of Siberia, and from the inhabitants of America, even to the ice of Labrador, and from the inhabitants of Africa, even to the desert plains of the Lesotho, and from all those who are Christians at heart among the millions of baptized people who cover the earth.

What am I saying? You can even draw the same testimony from those who are Christians in name only. In place of the faith they lack, they need only have the intelligence to understand that in sowing the principles of eternal life that I just pointed out to you, Saint Paul also liberally sowed the world with the seeds of culture, education, justice, order, freedom, and civilization.

Then, given the contemporary era, go back through the course of centuries and measure, if you can, the part Saint Paul had in all the good that has been done in the Christian world.

Measure the part he had in the religious awakening of our day—he who has always been the first to be consulted in all the religious awakenings of the peoples issued from the Gentiles. Measure the part he had in the Reformation—he who, in the library of Erfurt, awakened Luther, who was to awaken the church. Measure the part he had in the faithfulness of the inhabitants of Vaud[18] and the poor of Lyon—he who gave his name to the section of the Eastern Church of which they

---

[18] French-speaking province of Switzerland.

seem to be descendents.[19] Measure the part he had in the labors of Columbanus, Boniface, Patrick, Cyril and Methodius,[20] and of all the missionaries of Europe—he whose example they were only following and whose work they were only continuing. Measure the part he had in the conversion and growth of the church fathers—he who was the friend of Barnabas and Clement of Rome, the favorite master of Athanasius and Chrysostom.

Go back in time until you reach the solemn moment when his head falls at the gates of Rome. Go back to this moment which would have created such a great void in humanity if the letters of our apostle—his fourteen little letters, eagerly sought and transmitted from place to place—had not immediately come to complete the great efficacy of Paul's living word with the still greater efficacy of his written word.

And if you don't want to leave anything out, you need to continue following him into the obscure times that will follow on our heels. You need to try to appreciate the helpful influence that is still reserved for him in future generations, as it grows each day in depth and extent. You need to follow him until the prophecies that he himself wrote are completely fulfilled and the one whom he loved so much and waited for so impatiently has returned.

---

[19] G. S. Faber, *Vallenses and Albigenses*. [A.M.] George Stanley Faber, "An Inquiry into the History and Theology of the Vallenses and Albigenses (London: R.B. Seeley and W. Burnside, 1838).

[20] Saint Columbanus (540–615) was an Irish missionary in Europe; Saint Boniface (c. 672–754), born in what is now England, is the patron saint of Germany and was the first archbishop of Mainz; Saint Patrick (c. 387–493 or c. 460) was from Britain, served as a bishop in Ireland, and is considered the patron saint of that country; Cyril and Methodius were brothers from Greece in the 9th century who served as missionaries to the Slavic peoples, working to translate the Bible into what is now known as Old Church Slavonic.

Ah, who will calculate what the world owes Saint Paul, what it has owed him, and what it will owe him in terms of godly pastors, zealous missionaries, eminent Christians, useful books, and charitable foundations; in terms of examples of faith, charity, purity, and holiness? Who will even try to calculate it? All humanity should rise up and confess that among all its benefactors, whose names it delights to proclaim from age to age, there is none it proclaims with such agreement, gratitude, and love as the name of the apostle Paul!

PAUL'S WORK AND OURS

Two thoughts in summary: Without Paul in the world we would have the gospel confined perhaps for centuries within the confines of Asia and far from our Europe, which Paul, after Jesus Christ, made the center for the conversion and civilization of the globe. Without Paul in the Bible we would have Christian truth only half-revealed, the Christian life only half-understood, Christian charity only half-known, and the Christian faith only half-victorious.

PAUL IS BENEATH THE LORD

But that is enough time spent on the greatness of Paul's work. Let us fear even the appearance of giving to the apostle that which belongs only to the Lord. Once again, no idolatry! Between the apostle and the Lord there is the vast distance between imperfection and perfection, between the redeemed and the Redeemer, between man and God.

Moreover, as I have said and as you will see in the remaining discourses, far from wanting to hide Paul's weaknesses, I need them in order to place his example within our reach. It is thanks to them that he can say to us, "Become as

I am, for I also have become as you are" (Galatians 4:12). My plan is too serious for me to amuse myself by floating in the clouds of laudatory preaching. Thus I hasten toward the practical application of my subject. If I cause you to contemplate Saint Paul, it is for the formation among you of a people who imitate Saint Paul, a people who understand and carry out their work just as he understood and carried out his.

FAITHFULNESS, NOT AMBITION

He had his work, and we have ours; to each his own. I am not preaching ambition, not even spiritual ambition. I am preaching faithfulness. Far be it from me to give you a distaste for your work by proposing an illusory one for you, one that would be beyond your grasp and, moreover, is not part of your calling. For Saint Paul, the work of a Saint Paul, to which Saint Paul has been called by God and for which Saint Paul has been prepared by God. And for you, your work, to which you have equally been called and for which— do not doubt it—you have equally been prepared.

You do not have a world to traverse and convert, but you have something else to do for the glory of your Savior God. For you, it might be a flock to nourish with the Word of life. For you, it might be a family to support and to guide in the Lord's ways. For you, my sister, it might be a household to direct and young children to instruct. For you, young people, it might be studies to pursue in the interests of a future career, already known or still unknown.

Very well, whoever you are and whatever you might have to do, be content with the task that has fallen to you. Even while enlarging that task, should God give you the occasion to do so (see 1 Corinthians 7:21–22), aspire less to enlarging it than to fulfilling it, and to fulfill it—according to the wonderful expression that has become established in all the languages of men—is to leave none of its duties that your actions have not touched and permeated.

FAITHFULNESS, NOT IMPACT

Beyond that, we are poor judges of the impact God can give to our work. Saint Paul himself, in preaching the gospel or in writing his letters, was unaware of all the good that God was doing in the world through him. To understand would, perhaps, have been too great a stumbling block for one man's humility.

Let us only be faithful and leave the results to God. Whatever they might be, we will not lose our reward, which will be proportional less to the success than to the labor and less to the labor than to the spirit in which it was accomplished. Even if the results are nonexistent, we will at least have gained the ability to say, in the words of a holy prophet, "I have labored in vain; I have spent my strength for nothing and vanity; yet surely my right is with the LORD, and my recompense with my God" (Isaiah 49:4). But the results will not be nonexistent. The one who stands behind the language that I just borrowed from a prophet is not the prophet; it is the Messiah, the Messiah whose work, after a time of trial, was destined to cover and subdue the entire earth.

ADOPTING PAUL'S SPIRIT

Whatever the results, if each of you brings to your work the spirit that the great apostle brought to his, then the goal of this discourse will have been achieved. Do you want to? I'm not asking "Would you like to?" but "Do you want to?"[21]

---

[21] "Would like to" is conditional, and the implication is that our conditions are not going to be met; it is vague. "Want to" is definitive; a decision of the will has been reached; the matter is settled. In the French,

Everyone would like to do it, from the most unworthy, who give themselves over to evil without ever misjudging the claims of good, to the almost-Christians, who are touched by the beauty of the Christian life, yet still cannot decide to do all that God desires. These latter are sad, but sad like the rich young ruler, preferring to take that sadness as their portion rather than make the required sacrifice. I do not count on them, unless their hearts change.

Yet there are those who truly want to adopt Paul's spirit. (And there are more of them in front of me than one might think; perhaps more than even I, in my small faith, think.) They are the ones who, like Saint Paul, want to do what God requires, even though it cost them their most cherished idol, their most alluring pleasures, their most deeply rooted self-will. They are the ones who say to God in their prayers, "My God, you see my heart; here I am to do your will!"

Those, those alone make up the Lord's own people about whom I spoke to you in the beginning. It is on my heart to gather this people in spirit through the spoken word, until I or someone else more honored by God is allowed to convert that word into action. Then this people will be gathered into a visible body, to be a lamp set on a stand, a city set on a hill (Matthew 5:14–15).

EXPLAINING PAUL'S FAITHFULNESS

However, given the practical goal that I have in view, it is a small matter simply to excite you to jealousy through our apostle's faithfulness. We must seek the explanation of such active and rare faithfulness. How was Paul enabled to do all that he did? The subject is so extensive that examining this question will take up no less than three discourses. In moving backwards over the course of time, we will recognize in the

---

the basic verb is the same in both cases.

apostle's life a triple preparation for his work: his internal preparation (that is, his Christianity); his historical preparation (his conversion); and his natural preparation (his person). Thus we will, in turn, seek the apostle in Paul, in Saul, and in the transition from Saul to Paul.

It is only after tracing this entire pathway in the steps of the apostle that we can, in a final discourse, discern whether we are ready to follow him there and to enlist ourselves in the apostle-people for whom the Lord has reserved the work of raising up the church again and regenerating the world.

❋ second discourse ❋

HIS TEARFUL
CHRISTIANITY

HIS TEARFUL CHRISTIANITY

Acts 20:17–38

Now from Miletus he sent to Ephesus and called the elders of the church to come to him. And when they came to him, he said to them:

You yourselves know how I lived among you the whole time from the first day that I set foot in Asia, serving the Lord with all humility and WITH TEARS and with trials that happened to me through the plots of the Jews; how I did not shrink from declaring to you anything that was profitable, and teaching you in public and from house to house, testifying both to Jews and to Greeks of repentance toward God and of faith in our Lord Jesus Christ. And now, behold, I am going to Jerusalem, constrained by the Spirit, not knowing what will happen to me there, except that the Holy Spirit testifies to me in every city that imprisonment and afflictions await me. But I do not account my life of any value nor as precious to myself, if only I may finish my course and the ministry that I received from the Lord Jesus, to testify to the gospel of the grace of God. And now, behold, I know that none of you among whom I have gone about proclaiming the kingdom will see my face again. Therefore I testify to you this day that I am innocent of the blood of all of you, for I did not shrink from declaring to you the whole counsel of God. Pay careful attention to yourselves and to all the flock, in which the Holy Spirit has made you overseers, to care for the church of God, which he obtained with his own blood. I know that after my departure fierce wolves will come in among you, not sparing the flock; and from among your own selves will arise men speaking twisted things, to draw away the disciples after them. Therefore be alert, remembering that for three years I did not cease night or day to admonish everyone WITH TEARS. And now I commend you to God and to the word of his grace, which is able to build you up and to give you the inheritance among all those who are sanctified. I coveted no one's silver or gold or apparel. You yourselves know that these hands ministered to my necessities and to those who were with me. In all things I have shown you that by working hard in this way we must help the weak and remember the words of the Lord Jesus, how he himself said, 'It is more blessed to give than to receive.'"

And when he had said these things, he knelt down and prayed with them all. And there was MUCH WEEPING on the part of all; they embraced Paul and kissed him, being sorrowful most of all because of the word he had spoken, that they would not see his face again. And they accompanied him to the ship.

❖

PAUL'S SELF-PORTRAIT

In my desire today to explain Paul the apostle through Paul the Christian, I thought there was no more appropriate text to choose than the discourse he addressed to the Ephesian pastors. In it, Paul urges them to fulfill their task faithfully by invoking the faithfulness with which he has fulfilled his own. Thus he places himself personally in view (in the elevated sense of this phrase). He talks to them about himself, about what he has done, and about what he is. This is fortunate for our enquiry, for what more could we desire than to catch Saint Paul in the act of depicting himself through the traits that, in his own eyes, form the substance of his apostolic ministry?

THE APOSTLE-CHRISTIAN

It is true that he depicts himself as an apostle, and we wish to consider him as a Christian, but this difference, large with someone else, fades away with him. For him, the apostle is simply a Christian who is authorized by God to live exclusively to communicate his Christianity to the world and who is then equipped for this communication with certain supernatural powers. These powers are a grace of the apostleship but are not part of its intimate essence or distinctive strength.

For this reason, in depicting himself as an apostle, he depicts himself neither as an orator, nor as an administrator, nor as a man of learning, nor even as a recipient of the power of miracles. Rather, he depicts himself through his renouncement, through his charity, through his tenderness, descending even into that internal region where the Christian and the apostle merge in the inner man. In just a few lines, he delivers to us the secret of his apostolic life through the secret of his Christian life.

Yet these few lines are so full that I see myself constrained once more to make choices in this summary. Paul's doctrine, his faith, his charity, his zeal, his activity, his devotion, his patience, his vigilance—it is all there in this discourse. It is so short and yet so full of substance that it could be considered a kind of anticipatory funeral oration of his entire apostolic work. Among so many different traits making up Saint Paul's Christianity as he himself depicts it, I seek one salient trait that dominates the rest and comprises the unity of the portrait. I find this trait in the apostle's tears.

The Centrality of Paul's Tears

The more the indomitable energy of the greatest of the apostles seems to be in contrast with this poignant symptom of human weakness, tears, the more I am struck by the place they occupy in this scene in Miletus. Sometimes it is said that a man has tears in his voice; one could also say that Saint Paul has tears throughout his discourse, yet without those tears prejudicing (marvelous paradox of the gospel!) the Christian joy that breathes no less freely in it.

From the start of the discourse, I hear him recalling the tears with which his whole apostolic career is sown: "Serving the Lord with all humility and with tears." A little further on, he brings to remembrance the tears he shed in exhorting his dear Ephesians: "Remembering that for three years I did not cease night or day to admonish everyone with tears." Then, with his discourse ended and having taken great pains to contain himself for a few moments in order to pray, we see him mingling his tears with those of his listeners, because they are never to see each other again: "There was much weeping on the part of all."

THE NATURE OF HIS TEARS

Saint Paul's tears are not the tears of a soft or carnal compassion but the more serious and significant tears whose source lies in the very depths of both nature and grace. They will do better than just call forth a tear in our own eyes; they will awaken in our spirit more than one healthy reflection and will allow us to glimpse within the apostle's heart the inner and personal Christianity we are seeking.

Let us study them, then. Nor do they all have the same character. The first tears, dragged from him by the sufferings of his apostleship, are tears of pain and grief.[1] The second, the price of his pastoral concern, are tears of committed love. The last, shed at this moment in Miletus at the perspective of never seeing his Ephesian friends again, are tears of tenderness.

What an odd thought, you may say, to untangle Saint Paul's Christianity from his various tears! It can be as odd as you like, so long as it is valid, and its validity is all the more evident in that the apostle presents himself this way quite naturally, giving in to the impulse of his heart with no thought of putting on airs before anyone.

In addition, lest anyone fear that the vantage point I take is beneath my subject, the trait through which I am characterizing the apostle is one of those through which the Holy Spirit depicts the Master himself. Jesus had his tears, and all the same tears that Saint Paul had. He shed his tears of suffering when he wept in Gethsemane (Hebrews 5:7), his tears of love when he wept over the future of Jerusalem (Luke 19:41), and his tears of tenderness when he wept at the tomb of his friend Lazarus (John 11:35).

---

[1] The phrase "pain and grief" renders a single French word *douleurs*, which can mean either or both. It is often translated suffering, but another word for suffering (*souffrances*) is used earlier in the sentence.

TEARS OF SUFFERING

The first tears through which Saint Paul's inner man is revealed to us are his *tears of suffering*. Saint Paul is a Christian; he is not a Stoic. He doesn't pride himself, any more than his Master did, on stifling the expression of a suffering he cannot help but feel and that he could not hide without affectation. When suffering drags from a philosopher of antiquity the prideful exclamation, "Oh suffering, you will never make me confess that you are evil," he is only substituting a forced and hidden confession for the free and sincere one of a scream or a tear. There is no real strength except in what is true. Paul suffers; he weeps. And he wept much during his life because he suffered much.

EARLY SUFFERING

How can one speak of what Paul suffered without recounting his entire history from the time of his conversion? How much evil was done to him by the Jews, the only ones he names here, because everywhere he went they were either the authors or the instigators of all the persecutions he encountered!

He had hardly been converted at the gates of Damascus, and behold the Jews of Damascus would have killed him if he had not escaped from them by night, as his disciples "let him down through an opening in the wall, lowering him in a basket" (Acts 9:25).

When he arrived at Jerusalem, the Jews of Jerusalem, in turn, sought his life, and there was no way to shield him from their rage but to send him in haste to Tarsus.

In Paphos, a false Jewish prophet opposed his ministry. The Jews chased him from Pisidian Antioch. The Jews pursued him all the way to Iconium. The Jews had him stoned at the gates of Lystra. And these are just the first steps in his career. All that followed is consistent with this beginning.

ANTICIPATING THE HARVEST

Paul's whole ministry is a ministry of tears that fulfills all the bitterness predicted by the psalmist, so that it might also one day fulfill all the promised glory. "Those who sow in tears shall reap with shouts of joy! He who goes out weeping, bearing the seed for sowing, shall come home with shouts of joy, bringing his sheaves with him" (Psalm 126:5–6).

Paul anticipates the days of harvest through the power of his faith, and he triumphs even as he weeps. Yet he also weeps as he triumphs. He weeps while singing at midnight in the Philippian jail. He weeps while writing to the Thessalonians, "Rejoice always" (1 Thessalonians 5:16). He weeps during our discourse in Miletus while desiring to "finish my course with joy" (Acts 20:24, KJV). He weeps in Rome while intoning the song of departure. "For I am already being poured out as a drink offering, and the time of my departure has come. I have fought the good fight, I have finished the race, I have kept the faith" (2 Timothy 4:6–7).[2]

A MINISTRY OF SUFFERING

Now let us go back to our apostle himself. What a picture of suffering is seen in the summary of his life traced out by his own hand.

> Are they servants of Christ? I am a better one—I am talking like a madman—with far greater labors, far more imprisonments, with countless beatings, and often near death. Five times I received at the hands of

---

[2] Explained by Philippians 2:17. [A.M.]

the Jews the forty lashes less one. Three times I was beaten with rods. Once I was stoned. Three times I was shipwrecked; a night and a day I was adrift at sea; on frequent journeys, in danger from rivers, danger from robbers, danger from my own people, danger from Gentiles, danger in the city, danger in the wilderness, danger at sea, danger from false brothers; in toil and hardship, through many a sleepless night, in hunger and thirst, often without food, in cold and exposure. And, apart from other things, there is the daily pressure on me of my anxiety for all the churches. Who is weak, and I am not weak? Who is made to fall, and I am not indignant? — 2 Corinthians 11:23–29.

When he wrote this to the Corinthians during his long sojourn in Ephesus (Acts 19) and several months before the meeting in Miletus, Paul was scarcely two-thirds of the way through his course. He still had nearly ten more years to work—that is, to suffer—for his Master's name. What will he say when he has arrived at the end of his apostleship, when events have verified and perhaps surpassed the ominous forebodings that distressed him in Miletus without being able to shake him? "And now, behold, I am going to Jerusalem, constrained by the Spirit, not knowing what will happen to me there, except that the Holy Spirit testifies to me in every city that imprisonment and afflictions await me" (Acts 20:22–23).

Moreover, the One from whom the future hides nothing said it all on this subject in a single phrase, shorter and even more reliable than those of Paul. Right at the beginning, in sending Ananias to Saul, the Lord said to him, "Go, for he is a chosen instrument of mine to carry my name before the Gentiles and kings and the children of Israel. For I will show him how much he must suffer for the sake of my name" (Acts 9:15–16).

These last words, which I would willingly call Saint Paul's consecration sermon, unite his apostleship and his sufferings into one. If it is "through many tribulations [that] we must enter the kingdom of God" (Acts 14:22), then it is through double tribulations that we must proclaim it to the world.

TEARS THAT OPEN HEARTS

Yet the abundant tears with which the holy apostle is to sow his route will not water the earth in vain. They will make it fertile. One listens attentively to an advocate who has suffered for the cause he is defending. What surer pledge could he give of a sincere and deep conviction?

There is more. Independent of all such induction, suffering has its claims over man's heart. It exerts an influence, it wins an appropriate respect. The apostle himself, with an understanding of the human heart that breathes in all he says, appeals to this natural sentiment in writing to the Galatians. "From now on let no one cause me trouble, for I bear on my body the marks of Jesus" (Galatians 6:17).

Therefore, be no longer surprised that Paul so willingly returns to the recitation of his suffering. This is not the prideful satisfaction of speaking of self; this is a loving desire to persuade. Moreover, he had learned this tender pathway to man's heart from one greater than he. If the sufferings of Jesus Christ plead before God for grace toward sinful man, they also plead before man for the doctrine of a Savior God. Who has not sensed how much the ministry of Jesus Christ gains credibility in our minds—I should have said, in our hearts—through the terrible struggle in the wilderness that opens his redemptive career, through the series of unceasing persecutions that continue it, and, above all, through the bitterness of Gethsemane and Golgotha that marks its end? Our apostle thus truly entered into the spirit of his Master in writing the words—so embarrassing for commentators, yet so edifying for the simple—"Now I rejoice in my sufferings for your sake, and in my flesh I am filling up what is lacking in Christ's afflictions for the sake of his body, that is, the church" (Colossians 1:24). Here, the disciple's sufferings are made almost as necessary for the church's instruction as the Lord's sufferings are for her redemption.

Yes, my brothers, since the day when Jesus redeemed us on a cross, everything that is great and powerful and beneficial is also solemn. All the seeds of life and regeneration are sown in suffering and death. In order to stir even the least believing among you to salvation, do you know what I would like? I would like to have Paul climb into this pulpit, emaciated from fasting, worn out by fatigue, exhausted from watches, languished from prison, and mutilated by the rods of Philippi and the stones of Lystra. Imagine what an opening to his discourse this sight, those memories would provide! What weight, what savor they would lend to the least of his spoken words! What power!

Today's Comfortable Gospel

No minister of the gospel will ever attain such power if he is faithful in today's understanding of the term yet living in well-being—if he is a stranger to suffering, if he is drawing abundantly from the sweet things of personal, domestic, and public life, if he is honored, cherished, and sought after by all. These gospel ministers of well-being, alas, do we need to go very far to seek them? If we were something other than that, how would the current generation of God's children have given birth to us, how would it bear with us? Is this not the generation of well-being?

It has been noted that in our day, unlike previous eras, it is in the comfortable classes of society that the gospel has made the greatest progress. Let us add that in order to penetrate those classes, the gospel has been made in their image. The Christianity that is lived by the comfortable classes is as comfortable as they are. For in the end, what does it cost to be a Christian today—I mean an orthodox Christian, an irreproachable Christian according to today's concept of a Christian?

This used to be a dreadful question. What did it cost to be a Christian? Depending on the era, it might cost the sacrifice of well-being, or of fortune, or of honor, or of family, or of life. With us, let us agree, things are not so stark, and does not this difference, which has its merciful side as it relates to the Lord, also have a serious and almost frightening side as it relates to us, my brothers and sisters in Jesus Christ?

It is written, "Whoever does not bear his own cross and come after me cannot be my disciple" (Luke 14:27). Very well, where is your cross? What are the sacrifices, the bitter things, the humiliations to which your faith condemns you? In addition—above all, weigh this question—what are the pleasures, the delights, the vanities with which your gospel cannot be accommodated?

No, neither a life of frivolity nor a life of laziness can be allied with the Christian enterprise I have in view in these discourses. If you have it on your heart to contribute to the regeneration of the church and society, know for certain that you will never be able to do so without a serious, humble, and crucified life. Here we do not need another Jabez, whose prayer is, "Oh that you would bless me and enlarge my border and . . . keep me from . . . pain!" (1 Chronicles 4:10). We need a Saint Paul, "always carrying in the body the death of Jesus" (2 Corinthians 4:10).

Am I mistaken, my brothers, in thinking that more than one among you, running ahead of my exhortations, has secretly sighed after such a life of dying that is so bitter and yet so powerful? May a generation rise up that is more able than we are to respond to the holy work being proposed to us! And if, in order to bring it to birth, the earth that bears us is not sufficiently watered by the tears of the holy apostle, may it be so at least by the blood of the cross!

TEARS OF LOVE

"Therefore be alert, remembering that for three years I did not cease night or day to admonish everyone with tears" (Acts 20:31). I read this verse, I reread it, and I never grow weary of reading it again. In these *tears of love*, [3] I uncover the Christian in Saint Paul down to the depths of his inner man; I see what the apostle will be right to the end of his career. "For three years I did not cease night or day to admonish everyone with tears."

WARNING IN LOVE

What a way to warn people! Each bit of it strikes home. "Three years," without losing even one of the days he spent in Ephesus, from the first right up to the last—that covers the duration. "Night and day," rested or tired, in easy times or hard, "in season and out of season" (2 Timothy 4:2)—that covers the occasions. [4] "I did not cease," no letting up, no interruption—that covers the perseverance. "Everyone," not just the pastors of the Ephesian church, but its members—that covers the persons. Finally, "with tears"—that covers the love. [5]

---

[3] Love, as it is used in this discourse, translates the word *charité*, not the more common word *amour*. It expresses commitment or active concern more than a feeling. It conveys the idea of the Hebrew word *chesed* and the Greek word *agape*, which the King James Version of the Bible translates as "charity," an English word that has a different meaning today.

[4] "Making the best use of the time" (Ephesians 5:16). [A.M.]

[5] These last words, whose authenticity is not in doubt or debate, were, through some accident, omitted in the oldest of our French versions;

Try to picture the scene by putting yourself in the place of those whom Paul was warning this way. You are one of the Jews or one of the Gentiles from Ephesus who are beginning to pay attention to the gospel. The need here is to settle your mind, which is wavering between the world and God. Or perhaps you are one of the church members who have not yet really taken the gospel seriously or who claim to have reconciled it with the age. Thus the need is to win you unreservedly to Jesus Christ.

Here is the holy apostle who leaves you no more rest than he gives himself. He presses you during the day; he detains you on into the night. Don't go off complaining about his persistence, you ungrateful soul. He is only bothering *your* rest once, but he disturbs his own every night. When it is not for your sake, it is for others. Besides, no matter what you do, he will not let you go until he has obtained. . . what? Some favor, some kindness? Ah, the greatest favor, the greatest kindness that you could ever give him, the gift of being converted to Jesus Christ or of serving him with greater faithfulness.

You refuse him, you hide yourself from his pleas, perhaps you reject him, but before having done with him, look at him. He is weeping. He is weeping over the sins in which you persist, over the evil that your example does to the church, over the scandal that you give to the world, and, above all, over the future you are preparing for yourself. What do you have to say about this apostle in tears before you—I was going to say, in tears at your feet? The God whom he serves once summed up all that his apostle was supposed to be for him in the single phrase, "Behold, he is praying" (Acts 9:11). You, in turn, whom he evangelizes, can sum up all that he is for you in the single phrase, "Behold, he is weeping." [6]

---

an unfortunate omission, for the last brush stroke completes the tableau. [A.M.]

[6] See Philippians 3:18, 2 Corinthians 2:4, etc. [A.M.]

THE HEART OF HIS CHRISTIANITY

In the end, do not the tears you are costing Saint Paul enable you to read the heart of his Christianity? As for me, I discern in them a whole course in Christian doctrine or Christian practice. Far better than that, I find truth in place of doctrine and love in place of practice. Paul sees this truth so clearly that it causes him to sense a frightful calamity for you if you persist in rejecting it, and he feels this love so vividly that it makes your salvation almost as necessary as his own. What is this if not his beautiful definition of the Christian faith, "the truth in love" (Ephesians 4:15), augmented by an even more beautiful practical reality?

Here I address myself to those among you, my dear listeners, who charge our discourses with exaggeration. To them, the faith we preach seems too foreign in its maxims, too exclusive in its affirmations, too severe in its threats. I propose just one question to them and beg them to respond impartially. Did Saint Paul, whom you and I honor as the faithful guardian of divine revelation, understand the gospel the way you do or the way I do? To resolve that question, I limit myself to this one single trait: Saint Paul could not see his gospel rejected without shedding bitter tears. That is enough for me.

But what is this truth, I ask, what is the truth of the gospel according to this man who weeps as he urges you to receive it?

PURIFIED DEISM OR DIVINE REDEMPTION

Is Saint Paul's gospel merely a purified deism, proclaiming the existence of God and the immortality of the soul as its entire doctrine, the divine fatherhood and human brotherhood as its entire revelation, Jesus Christ living as a prophet and dying as a martyr as its only mediator? Or is this gospel really a completely separate religion, revealing strange novelties, proclaiming an unknown God, promising an inexpressible deliverance, requiring a radical change; is it merciful and yet terrible, as vast as the world, as high as heaven, as deep as hell?

There is no need to examine the apostle's writings and discourses, which are completely filled with "the good news" of an astonishing and unheard-of grace. You need only see him weeping at your feet. Yes, explain Saint Paul's tears to me if he had no other doctrine to bring to the world than yours. Would your doctrine cause weeping if it were not received? And what has it done for you that would compel you to do so much for it? Explain his tears if he proclaimed less than an incarnation, a redemption, a regeneration, a totally free grace, a Savior-God who is "the way, and the truth, and the life" (John 14:6)!

OPINION OR UNCHANGEABLE TRUTH

Is Saint Paul's gospel merely a somewhat solid interpretation, a somewhat established opinion that we should defend modestly against the interpretations and opinions of others, without absolutely affirming things, for fear of being charged with pride and intolerance? Or is this gospel really the one, incontestable, unchangeable, and eternal truth, which should be maintained despite all opposition with the inflexible firmness of a faith that is perfectly sure of itself?

There is no need to examine the apostle's writings and discourses, which consistently radiate a jealous faith that penetrates even to the most mysterious depths without losing anything of its marvelous precision. You only need to see him weeping at your feet. Yes, explain Saint Paul's tears to me if he had nothing more to bring into the world than a probable belief such as you would have done in his place. Explain them to me if he proclaimed less than the truth that alone is true, alone is necessary, alone is beneficial, and outside of which there is only waywardness, sin, and perdition!

EARTHLY TROUBLES OR ETERNAL TERRORS

Finally, does Saint Paul's gospel merely foresee somewhat painful exercises and somewhat difficult new trials waiting in the obscure developments of an impenetrable future for those who reject it? Or is this gospel really exposing for them the terrors of divine judgment, the dread of the wrath to come, the bitterness of an eternal punishment?

Let others discuss the exact sense of the word *eternal*. Let them research whether it is ever used for a finite duration, let them question text after text in the Scriptures, and let them examine the apostle's writings and discourses. You have no need of all that. You need only see him weeping at your feet. Yes, explain Saint Paul's tears to me, if he has at his disposition all the resources in which your compassion glories. Explain them to me if he does not have before his eyes the picture of some horrible punishment awaiting those who reject the truth or who turn away from it. Explain them to me if he does not glimpse ahead of them a frightful and inexpressible misery that exceeds all his conceptions of it or, to borrow his own powerful language, "a fearful expectation of judgment, and a fury of fire that will consume the adversaries" (Hebrews 10:27)!

SHARING PAUL'S TEARS OF LOVE

I just spoke on behalf of those who do not share our faith. You who share it, perhaps you are inwardly congratulating yourselves on being able to explain the tears of Saint Paul, whose gospel is also yours. Congratulate ourselves? Ah, that we might rather have reason to beat our breasts! Knowing how to explain the apostle's tears, we are all the more wretched for not knowing how to weep them. We challenge the heresy of explaining Saint Paul's tears apart from the truth he proclaims. Now let us allow that truth, in turn, to challenge us to explain his tears without the love that animates him.

Even with all the unheard-of novelty of his revelations, even with the unshakeable certainty of his faith, even with the vengeful fire that he proclaims to the impenitent, explain Saint Paul's tears to me if he does not join a divine love to this divine truth, if he does not desire your salvation as ardently as his own, if he does not live according to his Lord's saying, "You shall love your neighbor as yourself!" (Matthew 19:19, 22:39; Mark 12:31).

Also explain to me how you and I, who shed tears for our physical ills, tears for our family sorrows, and tears for our public calamities, can find their source dried up when it becomes only a matter of the loss of souls and the glory of God. Explain this to me if we are not just as cold and inconsistent as the apostle is loving and true to himself.

Saint Paul is weeping at your feet. What is this if it is not God's love living within a man's heart and converting the gospel into action, into evident truth, and into a real and palpable fact?

Irresistible Tears

Moreover, what power in those tears! Who could resist them? Could you yourself? Think about it.

Suppose you have lent an ear to the most eloquent, most pressing, most moving exhortations, yet you have not yielded. You have read solid treatises that are as well written as they are well thought out and in which the truth of miracles and the fulfillment of prophecy are demonstrated with almost mathematical precision, yet you have not yielded. You have listened to the Holy Scriptures, Moses and the prophets, the apostles and this same Saint Paul explaining the faith with a clarity arising from the very depth of things, a clarity that is its own argument, yet you have not yielded.

But suppose you were to see the Christian orator or the author of the treatise or the inspired witness of Jesus Christ, come into your private office. There, one on one with you, without any possible motive of human glory, he presses you to be converted, he begs you to have pity on yourself. Finally, at the sight of your stubborn resistance, unable either to stop you from being lost or to endure that you should be lost, he becomes flustered, falls silent, and dissolves in tears. Tell me, could you still not yield?

Alas, let us not go too far. Many, many have seen Saint Paul's tears and have not yielded, but for someone to resist the gospel preached that way, demonstrated that way, would he not have to carry around a stone instead of a heart?

WEEP FIRST FOR YOURSELF

People of God, when you arise in the midst of this wayward generation with Saint Paul's tears in your eyes, in your voice, in your heart; when you "take on the illnesses" of this great people that surrounds you "and bear their diseases" (see Matthew 8:17), then you will see if you do not gain a hearing.

But when will you have those tears? You will have them when you are the people of that which characterized Paul's apostleship, the people of truth in love. You will have them when you have ceased to be what you are today—soft in faith, weak in doctrine, cold toward God's rights, ignorant of his terrors, wavering on essential things while arguing about secondary ones. In other words, before you can learn to weep over others as Paul did, you must learn to weep over yourself!

TEARS OF TENDERNESS

Whatever impression the double memory of Paul's tears of suffering and tears of love may have produced on his listeners in Miletus, neither touched them as much as the *tears of tenderness* they saw streaming from his eyes at that very moment and with which they mingled their own. "There was much weeping on the part of all; they embraced Paul and kissed him, being sorrowful most of all because of the word he had spoken, that they would not see his face again" (Acts 20:37–38).

These tears of Christian friendship, while crowning the moving scene of my text, also instruct us in their own way. They complete for us the revelation of the apostle's personal Christianity and explain to us his influence.

A SENSITIVE HEART

The concepts of greatness and energy that even a superficial reading of the gospel causes us to associate with the name of Saint Paul could easily lead us to forget another trait of his character revealed by a more careful study of his story. Through a rare privilege of nature—or will I say, of grace?—Saint Paul joins together opposing qualities, tempering strength with gentleness. He bore one of the most sensitive hearts that ever beat under heaven. It was not just a warm heart but a sensitive heart, subject to tender attachments, lively emotions, and a ready tear. Thus his greatness had nothing haughty about it, and his energy had nothing hard.

What could be more affectionate than the apostle's language with his brothers from Thessalonica, his children in the faith? "We could have made demands as apostles of Christ. But we were gentle among you, like a nursing mother taking care of her own children. ... We were ready to share with you not only the gospel of God but also our own selves, because you had become very dear to us. . . . But since we were torn away from you, brothers, for a short time, in person not in heart, we endeavored the more eagerly and with great desire to see you face to face. . . . Therefore when we could bear it no longer, we were willing to be left behind at Athens alone, and we sent Timothy, our brother and God's coworker in the gospel of Christ, to establish and exhort you in your faith" (1 Thessalonians 2:6–8, 17; 3:1–2).

This applies to all those whom he has birthed into eternal life. They are all just so many friends whom he carries on his heart before God. The countless churches that he founded have not a single member who does not find his place in these prayers—prayers whose frequency is almost as astonishing as their fervor. One wonders where the apostle found the time (to speak only of time) to pray so consistently for so many people. Surely the inexhaustible tenderness of his soul plays a large part in the solution to this touching problem.

SPECIAL FRIENDSHIPS

Yet brotherly love does not exclude individual preferences. Too little attention is paid to the place that friendship, tender friendship, occupied in the life and apostolic work of Saint Paul.

In the interests of his ministry, Paul had voluntarily renounced the right he would have had "to take along a believing wife, as do the other apostles and the brothers of the Lord and Cephas" (1 Corinthians 9:5). He had not wanted to be a burden to the churches or to hinder his own liberty with the support and preoccupations of a family. But given the lively affections to which we see his heart prone, we can believe that he could not escape from the sweet bonds of domestic life without making a sacrifice that was perhaps greater for him than for many others.

There is, however, no sacrifice without compensation, and this very isolation in which Saint Paul took care to enclose himself opened within him a much easier access to the consolations and aid of Christian friendship. As proof of this, I need only cite the great number of brothers and sisters who are addressed by name at the end of most of his epistles and greeted by him, one by one, with the most delicate nuances of the most faithful Christian love. Though the apostle had voluntarily deprived himself of a natural family, his fraternal family was far more numerous and perhaps even more devoted than the natural family could have been.[7]

You have "Prisca and Aquila, my fellow workers in Christ Jesus, who risked their necks for my life" (Romans 16:3). You have "Andronicus and Junia, my kinsmen and fellow prisoners" who "were in Christ before me" (Romans 16:7). You have the "beloved Persis, who has worked hard in the Lord" (Romans 16:12). You have "Rufus, chosen in the Lord; also his mother, who has been a mother to me as well" (Romans 16:13). From this point of view, these chapters of greetings, which you perhaps skip over as devoid of general interest, would offer you an attractive as well as instructive study, causing you to delve into the private life of the apostle and into his personal relationships.

INTIMATE FRIENDSHIPS

That's not all. Among so many Christian friends crowding around him, Paul numbers a few for whom he keeps his most intimate attachment. There is Luke, his historian, so true yet so affectionate. There is Barnabas, his first fellow-worker, toward whom a brief separation could not chill him. There is Philemon, to whom he writes with an intensity of emotion that the pen of the most loving woman could not

---

[7] See Proverbs 18:24. [A.M.]

surpass. There is Epaphroditus, whom God restored in response to his prayers "lest I should have sorrow upon sorrow" (Philippians 2:27). There are Epaphras, Tychicus, and, above all others, Timothy and Titus—Timothy his right hand and Titus his left.

What mother ever wrote her son a letter more filled with concern than the second epistle to Timothy? The master's transparently affectionate language lets us read the inner man of the disciple, revealed through the pastoral—or should I say, paternal?—directions that are lavished on him. Can you not see Timothy giving in to the double pressure of a battered spirit and a languishing body and shedding abundant tears on the breast of his old friend? Paul is careful not to forget those tears; he knows all too well what tears are (see 2 Timothy 1:4). He lifts up the battered spirit through holy exhortations (see 2 Timothy 1:7–8, 2:3–6),[8] and there is nothing, even down to the languishing body, for which he does not have his vigilant and almost maternal instructions. "No longer drink only water, but use a little wine for the sake of your stomach and your frequent ailments" (1 Timothy 5:23).

And what can we say about Titus? If I depicted the apostle running from church to church after his dear disciple, his "true child in a common faith" (Titus 1:4), so as to find rest in his sweet company, you would willingly accuse me of exaggeration. Yet I would only be repeating what Paul himself said in an apostolic letter. "When I came to Troas to preach the gospel of Christ, even though a door was opened for me in the Lord, my spirit was not at rest because I did not find my brother Titus there. So I took leave of them and went on to Macedonia" (2 Corinthians 2:12–13).[9]

---

[8] Does it not seem that in this epistle Paul wanted to strengthen his disciple ahead of time against the painful news that would soon come to him (2 Timothy 4:6)? [A.M.]

[9] Compare this passage with 2 Corinthians 7:6–7. The consolation the

This is a man speaking, a weak man calling out for man's support. He is not like the unique man who is more than man and always equally strong in God, the one who could say, "You . . . will leave me alone. Yet I am not alone, for the Father is with me" (John 16:32). But if this is weakness on Paul's part, it is a charming weakness—if you will allow me to say so—and one which is even useful. The sparkle of such rare holiness would risk dazzling our eyes or causing us to doubt its reality if the man did not betray his existence somewhere.

A STRENGTH OF HIS APOSTLESHIP

Such is the source of the tears our apostle sheds at Miletus in taking his leave of the Ephesian pastors. I have called them tears of tenderness, but I could have called them tears of nature, for they arise from his attachment for his own family. Surely one of the first places in that family belonged to the pastors of a church where he had made more than one extended visit and where he had once lived for three entire years. Moreover, the characteristic these tears reveal in him doesn't just make up an interesting trait of his personal Christianity; it forms one of the strengths of his apostleship, a strength that operates in more than one way.

It operates by winning hearts to the apostle. Each one senses himself drawn to this man in whom the ability to love—the sweetest and yet most powerful ability to be found in man—has known extraordinary growth. The greatest obstacles the gospel encounters are those found in the will, so that the listener is biased in favor of the gospel when he is biased in favor of the one proclaiming it.

---

apostle finds in Titus' presence has a double cause: his friendship for Titus and his love for the Corinthians. [A.M.]

This strength also operates by multiplying the apostle's means of action. The fraternal family that gathers around such a loving master forms something like a holy phalanx surrounding him. Each member, assigned by his able general to the post that suits him, makes his personal contribution to the common effort against the enemy with an ardor proportional to the attachment he bears for his leader.[10]

This strength operates by using facts—the most decisive of proofs—to refute two prejudices that turn the leanings of a heart against the gospel. The first is that the gospel leaves no room for the preferences of friendship, whereas these preferences have been very well known in Saint Paul, to say nothing about them having been known in Jesus Christ himself. The other is that the gospel blunts human feelings and loosens human bonds, whereas Saint Paul's example, like that of Jesus Christ, shows that the gospel sharpens all true feelings and tightens all legitimate bonds.

But this strength of Paul's apostleship operates in an even deeper way, which is the only one I would like to pause over. The warmth and liveliness of the apostle's affections give the gospel he represents something of an air of simplicity and naturalness that makes it much easier for minds to submit to it. This requires some clarification.

A Gospel Suited to Our Humanity

Because the gospel has doctrines and maxims opposed to those currently in the world, it is commonly assumed that the

---

[10] This is perhaps one of the secondary reasons why Saint Paul is, of all the apostles, the one about whom primitive tradition has the most to say. Saint Paul's historians, who began as his fellow workers, speak of him through a need of their hearts, as a friend speaks of his friend. Who does not sense Saint Luke's heart beating beneath the simple and moving accounts in the Acts of the Apostles? [A.M.]

gospel has no relationship to the needs of our nature. It is said to be a fine theory, but one that could not become the law of humanity. For that to happen, humanity would have to be something other than what it is. Not only are public interests—commerce, industry, politics, the arts, literature—outside the reach of a gospel so little in accord with the world around us, but this gospel cannot even become the general principle for our private relationships, our personal feelings, or our moral life. It is not fully adapted to our inner man, since it opposes some of its instincts, even while satisfying others. In short, as is said today, the gospel is not *human*.

This thought closes many doors to the truth, because man cannot abandon his own inner depths. Thus the cause of the gospel is lost if it can only save man by denying humanity. Today, when the old objections of unbelief have, for the most part, lost their force, this one, on the contrary, is given more credit than ever and contributes to keeping many of the best minds far from faith. Yet this is nothing but a bias arising from the fact that our inherent and primitive nature is confused with our accidental and fallen nature.

No, the gospel—God's truth revealed to man—is no stranger to the bosom of humanity. It runs contrary only to its warped and perverted tendencies. It makes an alliance with natural humanity against fallen humanity, with man such as he should be against man such as he is. Because of this, even though the gospel appears foreign to unregenerate man, it is in perfect harmony with the true and permanent needs of human nature. It is to these that Jesus Christ universally makes his appeal, and his apostles, particularly Saint Paul, follow after him.

Because of this "naturalness," the gospel, preached and lived out as it was by Saint Paul, becomes comprehensible; it becomes visible, as if to the eye. Saint Paul's Christianity is essentially a human Christianity. The gospel has made everything new within the apostle's heart, while altering neither the general character of our species nor the personal temperament of the individual. Just as Paul strives to rid himself of all the evil in his old man, so he is also jealous to remain himself in everything that forms the purely natural core of his being. Thus the gospel exerts on him an influence that is at once both deeper and broader. Having become second nature to him, it permeates his whole being, taking on the character of an instinct that is irresistibly evident. He is seen to apply the gospel, in turn, to the smallest matters and to the greatest, always with the same simple ease.

On the one hand, raising himself to the highest regions of heaven, Paul "could wish that he himself were accursed" like Jesus Christ, "for the sake of his brothers, his kinsmen," the Israelites (see Romans 9:3). Or he sighs, longing for the moment for him "to depart and be with Christ, for that is far better" (Philippians 1:23). On the other hand, descending to the humblest earthly applications, he writes to the Christians of Corinth, regulating the organization of the church, the order of worship, the celebration of the sacraments, and even the dress appropriate for women. Beyond that, he is simply concerned for his books, which he cannot do without any longer, and for his only cloak, which he will need in the harsh season (see 2 Timothy 4:13, 21). In each case, it is always the Spirit of Jesus Christ that animates him, yet that Spirit has passed so thoroughly into his being as to have acquired an easy, natural control there that seems to belong only to Paul's own spirit.

Paul is a Christian friend, and accordingly a better friend. He is a Christian kinsman, and accordingly a better kinsman (see Romans 16:7). He is a Christian citizen, and accordingly a better citizen; a Christian craftsman, and accordingly—do not doubt it—a better craftsman (see Acts 18:3). He is the model of the Christian man, but he is no less the model of the human Christian.

A GOSPEL MEN CAN RECEIVE

This fact gives rise to Paul's influence on the human mind. The gospel, so inherently human in the apostle, addresses itself to what is inherently human in his listeners. "As in water face reflects face, so the heart of man reflects the man" (Proverbs 27:19).[11] The gospel finds in its listeners an ease of access it would never have had if it were not so completely "united by faith with those who listened" (Hebrews 4:2), having first been united with the one who proclaims it.

When Saint Paul proclaims the God of Jesus Christ to the Athenians as "the unknown God" to whom they have raised a nameless altar while not knowing him, you perhaps saw there only an ingenious introduction designed to catch the attention of a frivolous and spiritual audience. But this is more than an introduction; it is a truth. Saint Paul is so skillful on this occasion only because he is so true.

We are all Athenians, and no matter how much we have tried one idol after another, the true God, to whom our hearts aspire without knowing him, remains unknown as long as Jesus Christ has not been found. In the meantime, his place, which none other can ever occupy, remains empty in the depths of our heart until one day Jesus Christ comes to take that place and we cry out, "That is what I was looking for!" Thanks to the apostle's gospel, so natural and—if I dare say so—so personal, his battles are the battles of those who hear him, his experiences are their experiences, his feelings are their feelings. That is what draws them so strongly to him and through him to Jesus Christ, to whom alone he wants to win them.

---

[11] The version Monod quotes here has "heart responds to heart as face does to face in water." His point seems to be that just as we recognize our face when it is reflected in water, so we recognize our heart when we sense one like it reflected in someone else—in this case, Paul. Thus we are more receptive to the message this heart brings.

OUR SURFACE CHRISTIANITY

My brothers, our Christianity has an all too common flaw. It is external; it is a veneer. It is on us, but it isn't in us. Or, if you prefer, it is in us, but it isn't us. From our outer surface, where it resides, it has penetrated into our morning and evening prayers, but it hasn't permeated our domestic life, our office work, our literature, our commerce, or our politics. It hasn't been blended into our human existence, which is why it has taken so little hold on humanity. It seems to those who look at us as if, in order to receive our gospel, they would have to leave the world and separate themselves from the great human family.[12]

On the other hand, once they have dealt with Christians like Saint Paul, they will understand that the gospel alone is able to renew the depths of both man and society, being a stranger to nothing that is good and true[13] either in society or in man. They will understand that the gospel only opposes our superficial instincts in order more fully to satisfy our deep instincts. In this, the gospel is like the benevolent drill, moving aside the dry and sandy soil it encounters first on its path, but only to go seeking in the deeper ground for the clear healthy water that the overlying debris was hiding from man's use and from heaven's smile.

---

[12] This logic at first seems contradictory to our twenty-first century eyes. The Lausanne Covenant mentions two opposite problems that Christians can fall into: being conformed to the present age or withdrawing from it. While the former is the greater tendency in western societies today, Monod seems to be pointing to the problem of withdrawal. Thus the issue was not that the faith of many Christians was invisible, as is too often the case today, but rather that it was for show, an external "holiness" full of thou-shalt-nots that were perhaps not always adhered to in private life. Only when our Christianity causes us to be engaged with all aspects of life, but engaged in a totally new way, will we have a real impact on society.

[13] See Philippians 4:8. [A.M.]

WILLING TO SHARE PAUL'S TEARS

The holy apostle's tears have explained him to us. The power of his apostleship was in his personal Christianity, and his Christianity was a tearful Christianity. Weeping in suffering, he captivated people through respect. Weeping in committed love, he won them through love.[14] Weeping in tenderness, he drew them through the human simplicity of his gospel.

Christians, this has to do with us. In these discourses—do I need to repeat it?—Paul is for me only a means. My goal is you, or rather Jesus Christ in you. Far be it from me to have any thought of glorifying a man! The Lord alone is to be glorified, and Paul would not be Paul if he did not say with John the Baptist, "He must increase, but I must decrease" (John 3:30). No, I come not to glorify Paul; I come to humble you. I come to stimulate you through what one single man has done, because the infinite distance separating him from his divine Master has nonetheless allowed him to advance well ahead of us.

A true people of God must be formed. It will be at once the self-giving people of the cross, the devoted people of love, and the simple people of nature but of nature restored to its true self through grace. Let those who prefer well-being to the cross, egotism to love, and appearance to reality remain far removed from our holy enterprise. But you, people of tears, awake! In your turn, sow in tears so as reap with songs of triumph! Does Paul, who wept so much, now regret his weeping? Today *like* him; tomorrow *with* him!

---

[14] Here "committed love" expressed the word *charité*, which elsewhere is rendered "love." This is to distinguish it from "love" later in the sentence, which renders the usual French word *amour*.

third discourse

HIS RADICAL
CONVERSION

HIS RADICAL CONVERSION

Acts 9:1–22

But Saul, still breathing threats and murder against the disciples of the Lord, went to the high priest and asked him for letters to the synagogues at Damascus, so that if he found any belonging to the Way, men or women, he might bring them bound to Jerusalem. Now as he went on his way, he approached Damascus, and suddenly a light from heaven flashed around him. And falling to the ground he heard a voice saying to him, "Saul, Saul, why are you persecuting me?" And he said, "Who are you, Lord?" And he said, "I am Jesus, whom you are persecuting. But rise and enter the city, and you will be told what you are to do." The men who were traveling with him stood speechless, hearing the voice but seeing no one. Saul rose from the ground, and although his eyes were opened, he saw nothing. So they led him by the hand and brought him into Damascus. And for three days he was without sight, and neither ate nor drank.

Now there was a disciple at Damascus named
Ananias. The Lord said to him in a vision, "Ananias."
And he said, "Here I am, Lord." And the Lord said
to him, "Rise and go to the street called Straight, and
at the house of Judas look for a man of Tarsus named
Saul, for behold, he is praying, and he has seen in a
vision a man named Ananias come in and lay his
hands on him so that he might regain his sight." But
Ananias answered, "Lord, I have heard from many
about this man, how much evil he has done to your
saints at Jerusalem. And here he has authority from
the chief priests to bind all who call on your name."
But the Lord said to him, "Go, for he is a chosen
instrument of mine to carry my name before the
Gentiles and kings and the children of Israel. For I
will show him how much he must suffer for the sake
of my name." So Ananias departed and entered the
house. And laying his hands on him he said, "Brother
Saul, the Lord Jesus who appeared to you on the road
by which you came has sent me so that you may
regain your sight and be filled with the Holy Spirit."
And immediately something like scales fell from his
eyes, and he regained his sight. Then he rose and was
baptized; and taking food, he was strengthened.

For some days he was with the disciples at Damascus. And immediately he proclaimed Jesus in the
synagogues, saying, "He is the Son of God." And all
who heard him were amazed and said, "Is not this the
man who made havoc in Jerusalem of those who
called upon this name? And has he not come here for
this purpose, to bring them bound before the chief
priests?" But Saul increased all the more in strength,
and confounded the Jews who lived in Damascus by
proving that Jesus was the Christ.

THE TREE AND THE SEED

As the tree, so the seed. A Christianity as eminent as the one we recognized in the apostle must have as its starting point a conversion beyond all ordinary proportions. The conversion of Saul of Tarsus into Paul the apostle is the greatest event in the history of the early church after the deeds of Jesus and of the Holy Spirit.

A MODEL CONVERSION

Nevertheless, I do not want to dwell on the grandeur of the event; I want to dwell on its characteristics. For if Saint Paul is set before our eyes, it is not so that we might exalt him but so that he might instruct us. In examining a model conversion, I want to study the conversion that each of us needs in order to do his part in the work to which God is calling his people today. I find this model conversion in Saul of Tarsus.

With this truly extraordinary man, everything in both nature and grace is so strongly accentuated that the practical takes on almost the value of a theory. This is just one of the similarities between Saint Paul and his Master, and not the least astounding among them. One would call him, in turn, more man than other men in his natural state, and more Christian than other Christians in his state of grace.

We study the painter in the person of a Raphael because the heights to which such a genius raises art seem to be personified in the artist. We study the poet in a Dante because the heights to which he raises poetry seem to be personified in the poet. In the same way, we study the gospel almost as surely in the person of Saint Paul as in the pages of the book.

Using Paul, we study apostleship in the apostle, holiness in the saint, faith in the believer, and we also study conversion in the convert.

Therefore, let us untangle from Saul's conversion the characteristics of every true conversion—what it is, where it is going, and where it comes from; its nature, its extent, and its origin. In so doing, we will enter into Saint Paul's own thinking: "But I received mercy for this reason, that in me, as the foremost, Jesus Christ might display his perfect patience as an example to those who were to believe in him for eternal life" (1 Timothy 1:16).

What is Conversion?

What is conversion? Saint Paul's conversion answers this question with facts. Nowhere does our text (and here one recognizes the Word of God) tell us, "Saul was converted," but it shows him to us doing entirely new works, leaving us the task of concluding that his heart has been changed. In order to recognize this change, we need only take account of what he was before his conversion and what he is after it.

Paul, Before and After

After: Paul, an apostle of Jesus Christ; more than that, *the* apostle of Jesus Christ; of all the apostles, the one who worked the most (1 Corinthians 15:10) and the one who offered in his person the most complete model of the Christian faith and life.

Before: Saul, "a blasphemer" (he is the one speaking, or respect would never have allowed me such language), "persecutor, and insolent opponent," leaving grace nothing to latch onto except the fact that Saul "acted ignorantly in unbelief" (1 Timothy 1:13).

Thus we can well understand the natural surprise of his listeners in Damascus who, on hearing him confess Jesus Christ as the Son of God "were amazed and said, 'Is not this the man who made havoc in Jerusalem of those who called upon this name? And has he not come here for this purpose, to bring them bound before the chief priests?'" (Acts 9:21).

Suppose yourselves to be strangers to the story of Acts, and imagine that someone says to you, "There was a man named Saul who 'persecuted this Way [of Jesus Christ] to the death, binding and delivering to prison both men and women' (Acts 22:4). He 'punished them often in all the synagogues and tried to make them blaspheme' (that is, he tortured them), and 'in raging fury against them [he] persecuted them even to foreign cities' (Acts 26:11). He raced from Jerusalem 'toward Damascus to take those also who were there and bring them in bonds to Jerusalem to be punished' (Acts 22:5)."

Then imagine that someone says to you, "There was a man named Paul who served Jesus Christ with more ardor than any other. Like his Master, he lived and died solely for the good of the church. Cruelly tormented by the pagans and more cruelly tormented by the Jews, he 'did not account his life of any value nor as precious to himself' (see Acts 20:24), and he finished the most active and perhaps most devoted career the earth has ever known by crowning it with martyrdom."

Could you possibly think that these two men were one and the same? Very well, force yourself to make just one out of them; join them to one another as best you can. The difficulty that you will find there will give you a measure of what Christian conversion is and of the distance that separates it from all that is not Christian conversion.

MORE THAN AN OUTWARD CHANGE

Conversion is not simply a reform of one's conduct. We don't see anything that might be reproved in Saul's conduct. He boldly calls on the testimony of his entire people as to his "manner of life from [his] youth" (Acts 26:4). We could not represent him to ourselves as anything other than disciplined in his morals, honest in his business dealings, precise in his religious sacrifices, and liberal in his benevolent sacrifices—in a word, an honored and honorable man. But with all that, Saul was still Saul, and Paul had not yet begun.

Conversion is not simply a submission, even an inner submission, to the moral law. We cannot doubt that Saul was, in the deep and elevated sense of the word, a moral man, subordinating self-will to duty, even to the point of renouncement and sacrifice. He gives testimony to this in writing to the Philippians that "touching righteousness, under the law [he was] blameless" (Philippians 3:6). For the conscientious and believing Jew, this righteousness of the law was no small matter. Saint Peter calls it "a yoke on the neck of the disciples that neither our fathers nor we have been able to bear" (Acts 15:10). But with all that, Saul was still Saul, and Paul had not yet begun.

Conversion is not simply the acceptance, even sincere acceptance, of certain religious principles. Saul was a believing Israelite, a zealous Jew, a rigid Pharisee, strict among the strict.[1] He was submitted to the Scriptures, serving the true God, hoping in the Messiah, and as scrupulous in observing all the ordinances of Moses as he was ardent in defending them. But for all that, Saul was still Saul, and Paul had not yet begun.

Conversion is not simply the gradual development, the progressive improvement of all the good dispositions we just

---

[1] See Acts 26:5 and Philippians 3:5–6. [A.M.]

recognized in Saul. They might well have developed and improved, even over the course of a century, but all they could ever have yielded is what they already contained in seed form. Saul would only have continued to be Saul, and Paul would never have begun.

THE BEGINNING OF A NEW LIFE

Conversion is the starting point of a new life, quite the opposite of the former life in its general direction. This is what its very name implies, since it marks a turning back and a reversal of one's path. Through conversion, Saul doesn't become better; he becomes other. He is not more faithful than before to his principles; his principles have changed. That which he held as evil, he holds as good. What he called light, he calls darkness. He is experiencing personally what he is later to express so forcefully: "Therefore, if anyone is in Christ, he is a new creation. The old has passed away; behold, the new has come" (2 Corinthians 5:17).

A new seed, unknown and foreign, has been placed in the depths of his being. This seed is faith in Jesus, the Christ, the Son of God. Henceforth that which he was seeking through the law, he seeks only through grace; that which he was expecting from his own righteousness, he expects only from God's righteousness in Jesus Christ.

Moreover, behold his unadorned self-portrait, given in words that are so filled with truth and burning with love: "Whatever gain I had, I counted as loss for the sake of Christ. Indeed, I count everything as loss because of the surpassing worth of knowing Christ Jesus my Lord. For his sake I have suffered the loss of all things and count them as rubbish, in order that I may gain Christ and be found in him, not having a righteousness of my own that comes from the law, but that which comes through faith in Christ, the righteousness from God that depends on faith" (Philippians 3:7–9).

ENTERING INTO THE SAVIOR

There is Saul's conversion. There it is, recognized by its visible fruit; there it is, sought out in its hidden seed. Saul is converted the day, the hour, the moment when he recognizes himself to be wrong, unworthy, lost, and forever deprived of all righteousness before God, and when he substitutes the name of Jesus Christ for his own in all his hopes for eternal life. He is converted when he throws himself without reserve at the foot of the cross, as a poor sinner who has no other resource in the world than the blood of the Lamb of God.

Yet this same Saul, on the day, the hour, the moment when he is converted, enters fully into the spirit, the thoughts, the works of this Savior who has redeemed him. He doesn't simply cover himself with Jesus' name; he clothes himself with his righteousness, he unites himself with his entire being. As he no longer lives except through Jesus Christ, he also no longer lives except *for* Jesus Christ. Christ has become both the seed and the fruit, the beginning and the end, the alpha and the omega of his new life.

EVIDENT IN LIFE AND WORK

Very well, every true conversion, beginning as Saul's did, also finishes as his did. It begins with God seeing Jesus Christ living and reigning in a person's heart (2 Corinthians 13:5). It finishes with men seeing Jesus Christ living and reigning in his works (1 John 2:6). The contrast between the former life and the new life is so great that men are forced to say, as was said of Saul in Damascus, "Is not this the man" whom we knew but who was so different (Acts 9:21)? The converted person is so transformed that one can scarcely recognize him.

This man who is so intent upon his duties and so un-concerned over his rights, is he not the one whose sensitivity took offense at the slightest reproach and whose self-will grew irritated with the slightest opposition?

This man who is so gentle, so respectful, so serious, is he not the one who lost his temper at every turn, took God and man to task, and with profane flippancy mixed the Lord's holy name with the most vulgar, frivolous, and unworthy interests?

This man who is so generous, so quick to give, seeking occasions to do good, and seeing his fortune only as a deposit God has committed to his faith, is he not the one from whom it was so hard to extract even a modest contribution either for God's service or for the relief of the poor?

This man who lives a life of prayer, renouncement, holy activity, and generous devotion, is he not the one who took pleasure in the world's diversions—in its parties, vanities, and covetousness?

SEEK A CONVERSION LIKE PAUL'S

Act so that such statements can be made of you. Then your conversion will truly be a conversion. Then, too, you will have your appointed place in the labor of God's people. Then, but only then. . .

Oh, you who flatter yourselves as belonging to the Lord and who, I hope, truly do belong to him, do not stop until you have proven your conversion to every eye through the possession of a "new self," sanctified to where it offers a glorious contradiction with your "old self" (Ephesians 4:22, 24)! Speak no more of those insignificant conversions that barely touch a little head knowledge, a few surface habits, yet leave the supposed convert with his former tastes, expenditures, dissipations, stinginess, greed, and perhaps even his sins. Do not speak to me of them any longer in the presence of the conversion of Saul of Tarsus!

WHERE IS CONVERSION GOING?

Next, see where this conversion is going—that is to say, what influence it exerts in the world—and you will recognize what weight your own conversion will have in the eyes of men once it has the qualities we just recognized in Saul's.

THE IMPRESSION PRODUCED

The impression produced by Saul's conversion was as deep as it was extensive. This is seen first in the Jews of Damascus. "And all who heard him were amazed. . . . But Saul increased all the more in strength, and confounded the Jews who lived in Damascus by proving that Jesus was the Christ" (Acts 9:21–22). It is seen immediately afterwards in the Christian churches in Judea, as this news fills them with both surprise and comfort, stimulating them to glorify God because of him (Galatians 1:22–24). It will be seen later in all those throughout the entire world who receive word of his conversion and who find visible evidence there for the truth and power of the gospel.

The apostle was so aware of the fruit the world was to gather from his conversion that he made it one of the preferred arguments in his preaching. Of the five discourses preserved for us in Acts, there are two for which his conversion furnished the subject matter[2]—not to mention the repeated allusions that are made to it in his epistles.[3] With everyone he speaks to—the Jewish people, Agrippa, or the churches—he counts on the feelings that such a striking intervention by God on behalf of the doctrine of Jesus Christ must awaken in every honest soul.

---

[2] Acts 22 and 26. [A.M.]

[3] 1 Corinthians 15:9, 1 Timothy 1:12–16, etc. [A.M.]

He has good reason to count on such feelings. Apart from the resurrection of Jesus Christ and the coming of the Holy Spirit, gospel history has no testimony that equals the conversion of Saul of Tarsus. Every age senses it. There have been reflective spirits who yielded before this page of the gospel when they had yielded before no other. I can readily understand this. The least believing among you will do so as well, if they will but carefully and open-mindedly weigh the narrative of my text.

THE DRAMATIC CHANGE

Saul begins as a young Jew in whom his birth and parentage reinforce his religious prejudice. He belongs to the most rigid branch of the Pharisee's rigid sect. He is a disciple of Gamaliel, yet he is either more fervent than his master or led further by the new situation that Stephen's boldness had created for the gospel. Saul believes he is serving God in persecuting the disciples of Jesus Christ, even to death.[4] His initial effort is in the martyrdom of Saint Stephen, and the sight of this first blood only stirs up his fury. Having exhausted his work of "threats and murder" (Acts 9:1) in Jerusalem and Judea, he solicits from the Sanhedrin the favor of carrying it to foreign cities, just as Paul the apostle is later to seek the honor of carrying the gospel into regions it will not yet have reached.

Thus Saul, armed with official letters and messages, makes his way toward the populous city of Damascus, where the gospel has found ready access among the numerous Jews and the even more numerous pagan proselytes, especially the women. But as he approaches the city, behold, he suffers such an extraordinary change in his convictions and plans that, after three days of fasting, he is seen in this same

---

[4] See John 16:2. [A.M.]

Damascus substituting the office of Paul the apostle for that of Saul the persecutor.

There are the facts on Saul's moral outlook, removed from the supernatural circumstances that accompany them in Saint Luke's narrative and on which I will not dwell for the moment. How can these facts be explained? For in the end, in the moral world as in the physical world, there is no effect without a cause.

If the gospel is true, if Jesus Christ is the Son of God, if God has intervened, then all is clear. God does not squander his miracles, but one can easily understand that he might have had recourse to one in order to give just such a proof of the gospel and to provide himself with such a minister. However, if God did not intervene, if Jesus Christ is not his Son, if in the end the gospel is not true, I ask you, how do you explain the change in Saul?

INADEQUATE EXPLANATIONS

No one would dream of explaining it through self-interest, that great motivator of human action in unregenerate man and all too often, alas, in regenerate man. Saul's conversion too visibly compromised all of his interests. Instead of a brilliant career filled with honor, reputation, and fortune, we find Saul's name rejected by his people, we see his powerful friends turned into enemies, his family most likely armed against him, his person the focal point for persecution, and his life always threatened and set apart for eventual martyrdom. All this is so clear that it would be superfluous to dwell on it. Everything in Saul's conversion was unselfishness, renouncement, and sacrifice.

Would you, perhaps, consider explaining his conversion through influence, to which the most sincere are the most accessible? Could Saul, in a moment of great inner trouble, not have allowed himself to be persuaded by the wise and virtuous Ananias that his doctrine was wrong and the gospel true? Possible, though it remains then to account for the inner trouble that precedes Saul's encounter with Ananias. Possible again, though no human influence suffices to produce a change that is so immediate, so radical, and so exceptional. Ananias could have persuaded Saul, I grant you, if he had good reasons to present to him, or, in other words, if the gospel is true. On the other hand, one will never understand how a man as taken up as Saul with action, passion, self-will, and self-love would yield without good, solid reasons. Above all is this true of Saul, such a dynamic man, who was more used to exercising influence than submitting to it. And if he did submit to it—as can happen to even the most dynamic of men—if the position was taken, the mind won over, and the heart given, it would all be in a sense directly opposite to that of the humble trust of Ananias.

You might think of appealing to a third explanation as a bit more appropriate: religious exaltation. A man as ardent as Saul could, without thoughtful deliberation, pass from one fanaticism to another. Yet this hypothesis will not hold up against four minutes of reflection for anyone who recalls what the apostle Paul was. Paul had what was needed to satisfy his natural exaltation in his Jewish and Pharisaic faith, whereas in becoming a disciple of Jesus Christ, he set all that aside. Instead of entering into a new fanaticism, he broke with the old.

It would be strange fanaticism, indeed, if a man spoke, even on the most exciting occasions, in language marked by "true and rational words" (Acts 26:25).[5] It would be strange fanaticism for a man to take all his measures with the most consummate prudence, to be jealously careful for all his rights, even his social and civil rights, whenever they could serve the cause of the gospel or simply spare him unnec-

---

[5] See also 1 Corinthians 10:15. [A.M.]

essary pain (Acts 16:37–39, 22:25). It would be strange fanaticism for a man, in the interests of his ministry, to be ever striving to go to the very limit of the concessions that wisdom suggests and conscience authorizes, becoming weak with the weak, Jewish with the Jews, as one outside the law with those outside the law (1 Corinthians 9:20–22). Finally, it would be strange fanaticism for a man to spend thirty years pursuing the exercise of his ministry in this same spirit without ever awakening from his dream, even in the presence of martyrdom. Like his Master before him, Saint Paul takes as much care to draw back from his martyrdom as he later displays obedience in accepting it, once God's hour has arrived!

VERIFIED BY ITS FRUIT

No, I tell you, in spite of your best efforts, you will only find a reasonable solution to this problem through faith. Powerless as you are to explain the inexplicable change in Saul in any other way, your only other recourse is to try in desperation to deny the change and treat the entire narrative of my text as a fable. But don't you see that this would throw you into an even greater difficulty than all the other solutions? This conversion, which is the starting point of Paul the apostle, is the only way to explain all that he accomplished. Deny the change in Saul of Tarsus, yes, but then you burden yourself with supporting in thin air the apostle Paul and the immense movement he brought about in the known world.

This movement is a permanent marvel of which humanity is the witness, Asia and Europe are the theatre, and the renewal of history and civilization are the result. I who speak and you who listen are its fruit, if not through the faith we learned from our apostle, then at least through the countless benefits we owe to him.

Deny Saul's conversion, yes, but then also deny the conversion of half of Asia and all of Europe. Give Ephesus back to Diana, Athens to Minerva, Paphos to Venus, Rome to all the gods of its Pantheon, the pagan world to its dissolution and decadence, and our Gaul to its druids, human sacrifices, and barbarism!

Thanks be to you, oh my God, that in the midst of so many doctrines whose disciples can continue to believe only by gouging out their eyes, you have given me a doctrine to believe and to preach that I find to be ever more solid, ever truer as I delve into it more deeply. Its obscurities are only those shadows that our finite minds encounter in everything, and they cannot trouble the abundant and peaceful light from so many assembled proofs!

OUR CONVERSIONS VERIFY THE GOSPEL

To these proofs, Christians, each of you should add your own, as Saul of Tarsus did. I am not talking here about your discourses or even about your works. I'm talking about the mere fact of your conversion. If the evidence it offers pales beside what we just found in Saul as to its strength and clarity, let it at least not differ as to its spirit.

Let the change accomplished in you be sufficient to bear witness to the truth of the gospel and to confound the world "by proving that Jesus [is] the Christ" (Acts 9:22). Force those who look at you to say of your conversion, as we just said of Saul's, that it can only be explained by the truth of the gospel. Make it impossible for someone either to be unaware of your conversion, because of the precious fruit it gives, or to account for it through any interest, influence, or impulse. Let self-interest be excluded, because your selflessness and renouncement are too visible in everything you do; let influence be excluded, because you show yourself to be too independent with regard to man and too submitted to God alone; and let impulse be excluded, because you put too much maturity, too much prudence, and too much wisdom into all your works.

Struck by the apparently meager results that the preaching of the gospel produces today, we often ask ourselves what change would be needed to make it more effective. The most needful change is to transfer the preaching from us to you. As we are gathered here before God, you keep silent and we speak, but on leaving here the roles are reversed. It is up to us to keep silent and you to speak. Ah, speak; speak through the work of the Holy Spirit in you; speak the living gospel, more convincing than our preached gospel and also more visible out in society. Our preaching is but for a moment; yours is for the whole of life.

But where are the Christians who preach this way? Where do we look for those who would be an insoluble problem if the gospel isn't true? There are a few, no doubt—and may it please God to let his Spirit and favor rest on them—but how rare they are! Alas, how much easier it would be to find those who destroy our preaching and who convict it of error or impotence, because their conversion (if there is a conversion) is too easily explained by human reasons, without much mystery or grace!

HOW IS CONVERSION OBTAINED?

But this decisive conversion, where does it come from, and how is it obtained? We learn this as well from Saul of Tarsus.

GOD'S SOVEREIGN POWER

Conversion comes from God. It is less man converting himself to God than God converting man to himself. Never did God's grace burst forth more visibly or more gloriously than in Saul's conversion. He is converted as if in spite of himself. What advances did Saul make toward Jesus Christ? What advances did Jesus Christ not make toward Saul? It is when Saul denies, hates, and persecutes Jesus that Jesus appears to Saul, stops him, throws him to the ground, identifies himself, and changes Saul's heart.

This is a sovereign act, if ever there was such, and it is accompanied by language that is no less so. "He is a chosen instrument of mine" (Acts 9:15). "It is hard for you to kick against the goads. . . . I have appeared to you for this purpose, to appoint you as a servant and witness to the things in which you have seen me and to those in which I will appear to you, delivering you from your people and from the Gentiles—to whom I am sending you to open their eyes, so that they may turn from darkness to light and from the power of Satan to God" (Acts 26:14, 16–18).

Here you see that the same sovereignty God displayed over Saul in establishing him as a witness, he also wants to display over those to whom he sends Saul, by opening their hearts to his witness. It is only after being conquered by grace without having sought it that Saul begins, in turn, to seek that grace. "Behold, he is praying" (Acts 9:11). Then, in response to this prayer that God placed in his heart and in his mouth, Saul's deliverance is completed.

Here God's powerful and yet fatherly hand is revealed with amazing clarity to the apostle and, through the apostle, to us. It comes unmerited, unsought, unexpected, and unknown "to seek and to save the lost" (Luke 19:10)! Grace, election, foreknowledge, predestination—what language, what doctrine does not dwell beneath the simple facts we have before our eyes?

Ah, this is certainly the occasion to say what Paul later wrote to the Romans and what, no doubt, he wrote with his eyes fixed on his own story. "So then it depends not on

human will or exertion, but on God, who has mercy"
(Romans 9:16). Who knows this better than you, "Brother
Saul" (Acts 9:17)? As to human will, you wanted to stop the
gospel, and here you are preparing to spread it to the ends of
the earth! As to exertion, you were exerting yourself in
persecuting it, and here you are making your way toward
martyrdom!

GOD'S FREE GRACE

What's more, our apostle finds no words forceful enough
to extol adequately the free grace of God as it is seen either
in the work that was accomplished in him or in the work that
he desires to see accomplished in others. As to himself, "He
who had set me apart before I was born, and who called me
by his grace, was pleased to reveal his Son to me" (Galatians
1:15–16).[6] As to others, who has ever proclaimed the absolute freedom of grace more clearly, more boldly—one
would be tempted to say, more bluntly—than Paul? What
reader has not taken his turn at being shocked by verses such
as those in the eighth and ninth chapters of his epistle to the
Romans? "For those whom he foreknew he also predestined. . . . And those whom he predestined he also called, and
those whom he called he also justified, and those whom he
justified he also glorified" (Romans 8:29–30).[7]

Yes, conversion is God's work. It is a foreign seed de-
posited in our soul by a foreign hand. It is a new birth, a
resurrection from the dead, a second creation. No one can
change his own heart; he could just as well give himself life in
his mother's womb or raise a dead person from the tomb or
fling one more world out into space. Whoever desires this
new heart must ask it of God, "For from him and through

---

[6] See also 1 Corinthians 15:9–10, etc. [A.M.]
[7] See also Ephesians 2:8, Galatians 4:9, etc. [A.M.]

him and to him are all things. To him be glory forever.
Amen" (Romans 11:36).

MAN'S WILLING ACCEPTANCE

Are we then supposed to fold our arms and wait for the
miracle? Be careful not to believe that. And if you might be
tempted to do so through what you just saw happen in Saul
of Tarsus, disabuse yourself by looking more closely at this
same Saul of Tarsus. So far you have seen but one element of
his conversion: the divine, foreign element. There is another:
the human, personal element. If it is true to say that the
divine element was never more apparent, it is no less true to
say that the human element was never more perceptible. As
sovereignly as God operates in Saul, he only operates in him
as with a free, responsible creature, able to receive grace and
able also to refuse it.

The testimony that Caiaphas hears Jesus give about himself in the Sanhedrin is more solemn than the testimony Jesus
gives to Saul near Damascus (John 18), and yet Caiaphas'
conscience is not awakened. Why? Because Caiaphas is a
priest who is less fanatical than hypocritical. He serves only
his own pride and ambition. He questions Jesus only as a
formality, and he tears his garments only in a false show of
indignation (Matthew 26:57–66).

Balaam is stopped and subdued through a wonder even
more marvelous than the Damascus vision (Numbers 22),
and yet, in spite of the unwilling obedience dragged from his
lips, he holds on to the unregenerate heart he had before he
was "rebuked for his own transgression [by] a speechless
donkey [that] spoke with human voice" (2 Peter 2:16). Why
again? Because Balaam is a lover of money "who loves gain
from wrongdoing" (see 2 Peter 2:15), who makes a career
and a commodity out of prophecy, and whose only concern,

even in his prayers, is lulling his conscience to sleep so that it
will let him give himself over to his thirst for gold.

In a word, the problem is that neither Caiaphas nor
Balaam has within him an upright heart. Without such a heart
God could, no doubt, still act, because he is the master of
everything, yet without such a heart it is well outside the
normal workings of his providence to do so. I will go further;
without such a heart we have no reason to expect him ever to
act. Every conversion is a covenant. In the heart that God's
grace wants to renew, it needs to find something that perhaps
doesn't call out to grace but that at least gathers it in, even if
that something is only a void ready to receive it. An abiding
difference between material creation and spiritual creation is
that in the second, man has a part to play, if not by action
then at least by consent. A father of the church[8] has rightly
said that God, who created us without our consent, does not
want to save us without our cooperation.

An Upright Heart

Very well, this upright heart (which may still be allied
with great misconceptions) is in Saul. It is in Saul the "blasphemer, persecutor, and insolent opponent" (1 Timothy
1:13); it is in Saul guarding the cloaks of Stephen's murderers
and giving support to his death.

You remember Nathanael. He was filled with reservations about Jesus Christ, but his reservations gave way at
his first encounter with him, because they were only the
unconscious weakness of "an Israelite indeed, in whom there
is no deceit!" (John 1:47). Saul is a Nathanael, but a giant
Nathanael. God allowed his prejudices to take on alarming
proportions so that the truth that was to conquer them
would, of necessity, see colossal growth. Nathanael would

---

[8] Saint Augustine.

have yielded ten times before a sight such as Stephen's death. Saul did not yield. Instead, his anger was all the more inflamed against the one on whom Stephen called with so much faith and in whom he fell asleep with so much peace.

Yet, for all we know this sight might have given rise in Saul's heart to an initial uneasiness, an initial healthy doubt. For all we know this uneasiness, this doubt, pushed away at first like a troubling temptation and perhaps translated into bitterness and violence, might have paved the way for the Damascus scene.

Saul, Stephen's murderer; Saul, Stephen's disciple and successor. Oh, the depths and the mercy of this!

Whatever the case, everything Paul said about himself shows him before his conversion to be an opinionated but convinced Jew, an ardent but sincere Pharisee (Philippians 3:5, Acts 26:4–5), serving God, "as did [his] ancestors, with a clear conscience" (2 Timothy 1:3). Even in the journey to Damascus, can you not untangle from Saul's sinister and criminal waywardness the kind of blind desire to serve God to which Jesus gave such balanced testimony (John 16:2)? At the very moment the transition is occurring from hatred to obedience and from Saul to Paul, we hear these words, worthy of Nathanael, "What shall I do, Lord?" (Acts 22:10).

To whom do these words belong? Is it still to Saul, or is it already to Paul? They belong to both. Do not think that the passage from Saul to Paul was abrupt and without transition. There is Paul within Saul, and there is Saul within Paul. There is an intimate, secret point, "hidden from the eyes of all living and concealed from the birds of the air" (Job 28:21), where grace is joined to nature, God's work to man's work, new life to former life, Paul the apostle to Saul of Tarsus. This point is the feeling that causes him to say, "What shall I do?" but to say it in the light of the moment.

Yesterday it was the God of Moses; today it is the God of Jesus Christ, dimly perceived for the first time.

IGNORANCE VERSUS RESISTANCE

Do not accuse this commentary of being rash. I uphold it with good authority, the authority of Saint Paul. "I thank him who has given me strength, Christ Jesus our Lord, because he judged me faithful, appointing me to his service, though formerly I was a blasphemer, persecutor, and insolent opponent. But I received mercy because I had acted ignorantly in unbelief" (1 Timothy 1:12–13).

This statement is quite remarkable, deep, and instructive. It is not that Saint Paul's unbelief about Jesus Christ and the ignorance in which it kept him gave him a right to divine mercy. Rights! Who attributed them to himself less than our apostle, and where does he attribute them to himself less than here? Rights! He recognizes none for himself but perdition. He knows himself to be the foremost of sinners (1 Timothy 1:15), whom Jesus Christ has saved expressly so "that in me, as the foremost, [he] might display his perfect patience" (1 Timothy 1:16).

The point is that this ignorance left him accessible to grace, whereas a conscious and voluntary resistance would have invincibly armed his heart against it. Saul doesn't merit the conversion by his ignorance. Rather, because he is ignorant, he is not among those impenitent and hardened souls for whom grace itself has no more resources—all its resources having been tried and exhausted without yielding fruit (Hebrews 6:1–4). Saul, all Saul that he is, seeks God in his own fashion, as if "feeling his way" (see Acts 17:27) through the darkness of the law. He is almost like Luther, who was later to seek God in his cell in Erfurt through mortifications of the flesh and penances. That is why God placed a Bible on Luther's pathway and Jesus Christ on Saul's.

DON'T WAIT FOR A MIRACLE

If then you desire to have a share in Saul's grace, seek God, without waiting for the miracle for which he in no wise waited and which he would not have obtained had he waited for it. Like Saul, bring to God a heart jealous to know him and careful to obey him. Then, though you be, if possible, as blind as he was, God will reveal himself to you, and you will experience, in your turn, the truth of the Savior's word, "If anyone's will is to do God's will, he will know whether the teaching is from God or whether I am speaking on my own authority" (John 7:17).

Compare this saying with the superficial one routinely peddled by a world as uncaring about truth as it is about holiness: "Faith is less important than good faith." [9] Do I need to point out the vast difference between the two? The good faith or sincerity of which Jesus speaks and that animates Saul is a good faith that seeks God and that, once he is found, follows him. It is a good faith that does not happen without a beginning of faith.[10] It is a good faith, in short, that is pursued in good faith. Bring, I tell you, a heart that seeks God, a heart resolved to do anything to find him, to suffer anything to please him. Then, count on his grace to accomplish his work in you and to prepare you for your own work.

Do you have this heart? If so, then all will go well; if not, then don't flatter yourself. You might live a century, listening to the best discourses each Sunday, reading the divine Scriptures every day, surrounded by the most faithful Christians, and you would never be converted. Nothing, no, nothing in the world can substitute for the simplicity of an upright heart; nothing, either in nature or in events or in men or in God

---

[9] I.e., "having faith in God" vs. "acting in good faith," with integrity and an intention to follow through with one's commitments.
[10] See Hebrews 11:6. [A.M.]

himself. God—if you will put up with the boldness of my language—God cannot convert those who do not have an upright heart, any more than Jesus "could do" mighty works on behalf of those who did not believe (Mark 6:5–6). He cannot because he does not want to, and he does not want to because his holiness does not allow him to want to.

THE SEED AND THE TREE

I said at the beginning: As the tree, so the seed. I say in concluding: As the seed, so the tree. Conversion, true conversion, radical like Saul's, demonstrating the gospel like Saul's, the fruit of grace in an upright heart like Saul's—such a conversion is the nerve fiber of the holy war in which I aspire to enroll you. Give me such conversions, and I will give you a "people [who] will offer themselves freely" (Psalm 110:3) for God's service.

Oh, you who have previously lived far from the Savior and from his grace but who aspire to belong to him, "today, if you hear his voice, do not harden your hearts!" (Hebrews 3:7–8, 3:15, 4:7).

But you above all, brothers and sisters, who have known this grace, who have served this Savior, but who do not find in yourselves what is needed to provide for the new course to which I call you; you who are Christians but have nothing of Paul in your Christianity, who are converted but have nothing of Saul in your conversion—go back, retrace your steps, return to your beginnings! Plunge yourselves anew in the fountain of life! In order to make provision for your Christianity, start by converting your conversion.

❋

fourth discourse

His Personal Weaknesses

His Personal Weaknesses

2 Corinthians 12:5–10

On my own behalf I will not boast, except of my weaknesses. Though if I should wish to boast, I would not be a fool, for I would be speaking the truth. But I refrain from it, so that no one may think more of me than he sees in me or hears from me. So to keep me from being too elated by the surpassing greatness of the revelations, a thorn was given me in the flesh, a messenger of Satan to harass me, to keep me from being too elated. Three times I pleaded with the Lord about this, that it should leave me. But he said to me, "My grace is sufficient for you, for my power is made perfect in weakness." Therefore I will boast all the more gladly of my weaknesses, so that the power of Christ may rest upon me. For the sake of Christ, then, I am content with weaknesses, insults, hardships, persecutions, and calamities. For when I am weak, then I am strong.

❉

THE PROBLEM OF WEAKNESS

I am assuming, my dear listener, that after my previous discourses on the apostle Paul you are convinced you have a work to do both for the glory of God and for the good of men. I am assuming that you are clearly discerning this work and that you have seriously resolved to accomplish it. There is, however, one thing that troubles you: your task is beyond your abilities. On the one hand, lacking a natural aptitude, you are not suited to it, so that with sadness you note your physical, intellectual and moral weaknesses. On the other hand, not having used your time well, you are not trained for it, so that with bitterness you count the lost hours, missed opportunities, neglected resources, and buried talents.

This is enough to give you over to discouragement. Yes, to discouragement, that characteristic trait of our era; to discouragement, the devil's subtle tactic against those to whom he would not dare to mention despair or unbelief. And what does he care about words, provided one turns things over to him?

YOUTH'S SENSE OF WEAKNESS

Even youth are subject to such debilitating thoughts, and this discourse is addressed especially to youth. In these days of crisis and transition, are not the young the hope of the church, just as they are the hope of society? The generation to which your speaker belongs was once chosen to bring about the religious awakening of our century, yet today perhaps it is too weak or too busy to impart the new stimulus for which we all long and of which we see so many harbingers.

Young Christians, we are counting on you in the Lord far more than on ourselves, and our sweetest yet most earnest ambition is to shape you for the great task we glimpse ahead of you. You glimpse it yourselves. The greater it is, the more it draws you—I delight to bear you this testimony—but also, the greater it is, the more it terrifies you, and the most reflective among you are the first to say, "I am neither fit nor skilled for it."

Alas, need one have lived so many years to beat his breast on comparing what he is with what he could be, what he has done with what he could have done? Besides, what is more contagious than discouragement? It is the order of the day among contemporary youth. The pleasant elasticity of this age group bends beneath the weight of this common pre-occupation. One would say that they are burdened with the years ahead of them, just as one is ordinarily burdened with those behind him. This again is among "the signs of the times" (Matthew 16:3).

SAUL'S SENSE OF WEAKNESS

Do you think, my young friends, that the young Saul was spared from the thoughts that trouble you? Called to apostle-ship as soon as he was converted, he was to "carry [the Lord's] name before the Gentiles and kings and the children of Israel" (Acts 9:15). In measuring the calling that fell to him against the natural or acquired strengths that were his lot, do you think that he rested complacently convinced that he had the required aptitude and the desired training? Oh, no! You don't recognize the godly apostle in those thoughts. He had his battles, his sadness, his bitterness, just as you do and per-haps more than you do. He said to himself more than once, "Who is sufficient for these things?" (2 Corinthians 2:16). Perhaps he even went so far as to say with Moses, "Oh, my Lord, please send someone else" (Exodus 4:13).

Yet he found peace in looking to God, whose "thoughts are not our thoughts, neither are his ways our ways" (see

Isaiah 55:8). He understood that God, "who had set him apart before he was born, and who called him by his grace" (see Galatians 1:15), would not have chosen him without aptitude or called him without training. Such as he was and given the work God appointed for him, Saul was far better prepared by God than he could have prepared himself, even had he been able to foresee that work.

This preparation has two parts. The first is a preparation of strength—that is, of his natural gifts, which he henceforth consecrates to the Lord's service. The second is a preparation of weakness—that is, of his infirmities, which constrain him to take refuge in the Lord's grace alone. He is indifferently occupied with the first, but the second, by contrast, holds a large place in his discourses and letters. My text sums up all that he says elsewhere on this subject in the few words that I call Saint Paul's motto: "When I am weak, then I am strong" (2 Corinthians 12:10).

Astonishing thing! The greatest of all men has been strengthened for the greatest of all undertakings through what? Through his weakness. This is not a clever paradox; it is the simple truth. You are going to see it, so that you may learn that you yourselves, such as you are, are prepared for whatever work God has appointed for you. You will learn that what you call your most overwhelming weaknesses can become your most fruitful resources.

THE PREPARATION OF STRENGTH

There was with Paul a preparation of strength. By this I mean that he had certain advantages, natural or acquired, that God, who is their source, used to further his plan and serve his purposes.

Saul of Tarsus was no ordinary man, nor had God enriched him without a purpose. "All things are [his] servants"

(Psalm 119:91), and surely the diverse talents of men are no exception to this sovereign rule. Saint Paul's story, his writings, his discourses all reveal even to the superficial observer, a rare combination of the most exquisite and most cultivated gifts. These gifts are evident even in the presence of inspiration, which directs someone's nature without destroying it and controls it without effacing it.

EXTRAORDINARY NATURAL GIFTS

Consider Paul's gifts of character: an indomitable energy, an invincible perseverance, a will that nothing can take by surprise when he is undertaking a venture and nothing can demoralize in its execution.

Consider his emotional gifts: a liveliness of spirit and heart that shows itself in even the smallest things; a warmth of affection that raises friendship to the level of family ties; a compassionate tenderness that takes up the interests, the needs, the battles, and even the weaknesses of others; an anointed language that will stir even the most intimate depths of the soul.

Consider, above all, his intellectual gifts: a power of abstraction that the most thoughtful reader despairs of following to its end; a perceptiveness that is at once so delicate and so strong that it finds nothing to be inaccessible; a fertility of thought that the tenth reading does not exhaust any more than the first one does; a rich yet concise language that encloses a world of things in a single page of words and becomes obscure only because it penetrates beneath the soil trampled by the ordinary; a vigorous genius tempered by an amiable grace that sows lively or touching remarks in abundance. All this is ripened through long study, whose main object is the literature and theology of Judaism but which excludes neither the letters nor the laws nor the mores of other nations.

FROM GOD, FOR GOD'S GLORY

All this is but an imperfect sketch of the great apostle, and who would dare flatter himself that he has painted such a man without either weakening the lines of the portrait or exaggerating them? Whatever the case, Saint Paul had at his disposal uncommon human resources; it would be unnatural to ignore this. And why ignore it? Is it in the interests of God's glory that we close our eyes to the gifts from his hands? Certainly not, provided we relate their source to God's grace and their use to his glory. In the same spirit, this same Saint Paul said, "Who sees anything different in you? What do you have that you did not receive? If then you received it, why do you boast as if you did not receive it?" (1 Corinthians 4:7).

In this regard, let us listen to the knowledgeable and godly Neander, who has made one of most thorough studies of the history of the early church.

> Divine grace is pleased, as Saint Paul himself observed,[1] to choose at the outset foolish things to shame the wise, weak things to shame the strong, and things that are low and despised in the world, even things that are not, to bring to nothing things that are. That is why Christ took as his first disciples, not the wise and great of this world, but simple, ignorant, coarse men, sinners and tax collectors. They didn't even have eminent natural faculties. Receiving everything from him and bringing him nothing, they could expect nothing but his grace alone.
>
> Yet we then need to recognize that the God of grace is also the God of nature. The admirable strengths

---

[1] 1 Corinthians 1:27–29. [A.M.]

with which he provided man in creating him are far from being alien to the establishment and growth of God's spiritual reign (which is the final goal of all his works and his first claim to glory). Rather, they must be constantly applied to this end or else they risk missing their highest purpose. Thus it has entered into the special plans of divine wisdom that the work begun by sinners and tax collectors was continued by a mind trained in the art of thinking in the schools of Judaic wisdom. Without contradiction, had Paul so desired, he would have shone among the first ranks of sages and orators of all centuries and had no cause to yield to any of the masters of thought or speech of whom ancient Greece could boast.[2]

What Neander says here of Saint Paul can be equally said of all God's great servants. Each had an element of suitable strength and natural aptitude, to which God, in the counsels of his providence, had given its correct place. This one had the gift of speaking; that one, the gift of writing; a third, the spirit of organizing and carrying out; a fourth, the art of influencing men; another, something else. You too, whoever you are and whatever it pleases God to give you to do, do not doubt that you have received the measure of strength and ability that is necessary for your work. Here, as elsewhere, what matters is not seeing but believing. True faithfulness does not consist in being aware of our gifts any more than true humility consists of being ignorant of them. We will be both faithful and humble in taking them as God made them and consecrating them to his service, convinced that he who calls us is also the one who prepares us.

---

[2] Adolphe Monod does not give a precise source for this quotation. The author is most probably August Neander (1789–1850), a church historian.

THE NECESSITY OF WEAKNESS

Nonetheless, this preparation of strength is not the main, distinctive preparation of our apostle. His distinctive preparation—the one that gives this great life its enigma, the one that makes Saint Paul a Saint Paul—is a preparation of weakness. If necessary, Saint Paul could have done without his eminent gifts. He could have gotten away with throwing himself even more fully, if it were possible, into the hands of the God who called him and who, in calling him, had tacitly pledged to prepare him.

On the other hand, without his weaknesses, he would no longer have been himself. Without them he would have stopped at the level of an Apollos or a Barnabas or a Timothy. He would not have attained the level of Saint Paul, because he wouldn't have been, in the highest sense of the word, the man of faith. The point is that, in spite of all the promises made to faith, we are always more or less weakened by a remnant of self-reliance, just as we are always more or less troubled by a remnant of self-righteousness, which even the most humble drag with them wherever they go. Our own miserable strength, our own talent, our own eloquence, our own knowledge, our own influence—all of that forms within us a favorite little sanctuary, which our jealous pride keeps closed to God's strength, so as to maintain a last refuge for itself.

Yet, if we could finally become truly weak and absolutely despairing of ourselves, then God's strength, spreading throughout our inner man and infiltrating even our most secret recesses, would fill us "with all the fullness of God" (Ephesians 3:19). With man's strength having been exchanged for God's strength, "nothing will be impossible for" us (Matthew 17:20) because "nothing will be impossible with God" (Luke 1:37). This is the invaluable service that Paul's weakness did for him and that no strength would ever have done. Sensing himself to be deprived of all human strength, he gave himself without reservation to the working of divine strength, and God enriched that strength, the only true strength, all the more willingly because, given Paul's disposition of spirit, he had no fear that Paul would draw glory to himself. Blessed weakness that makes the one more suited to ask and the other more eager to give! That is Saint Paul's secret power. That is also what will be the basis of your power, if you are willing to enter into his spirit.

HIS EDUCATIONAL WEAKNESS

The first weakness that the converted Saul of Tarsus must recognize is *an educational weakness*, which is all the greater because it resides within the intellectual and moral man.

LEGALISTIC RIGHTEOUSNESS

What is Saul henceforth called to do, and how has he been trained for it up to this point? As an apostle, but to the Gentiles, he cannot hope to make them accept the gospel, which is so new to them, except by offering it to them freed from everything that is particularly Jewish. It must be reduced to its intimate, universal, and permanent essence. Justification through faith, without the works of the law— accessible to the Greek as well as to the Jew, and necessary to the Jew as well as to the Greek—this is the theme born of Saint Paul's apostleship, and it is totally unlike the legal righteousness that the Jew prided himself on being the only nation to possess.

Now, think what an education Saul had for proclaiming this totally free grace to the world! He has heretofore been a Jew among the Jews, a Pharisee among the Pharisees, aspiring only to the legal righteousness that henceforth he is charged with combating, and knowing only the false logic of the synagogue that he is going to find everywhere along his path! Can the mind, the heart, and the conscience of the new apostle possibly be stripped of these firmly engrained prejudices and habits, so that not even a vague shadow of them remains on his words to obscure the pure light of his gospel?

Used by the Holy Spirit

Count on God's Spirit to remove from him every vestige of the memories and impressions of the past. Rest assured, the Spirit can do it, will do it, has done it. But recognize with me that once this inner release has occurred, the new doctrine of grace will find in Paul a more intelligent and devoted proponent; it will be revealed more clearly to him through the very contrast it presents with his regrettable past.

What happens here to Saul is something analogous to what was to happen fifteen centuries later to Luther, the Saul of the Reformation.

Why does God want the young professor of Wittenberg to leave his fine genius imprisoned in the bizarre and sterile scholasticism of the Middle Age? Because in him God is preparing one who is to renew theology. Through the emptiness and pomp in scholasticism, Luther is to learn to taste all that is true and solid and healthy in the wisdom of the Scriptures when they are welcomed with an honest heart and sound judgment.

Why again does God want the young monk of Erfurt fruitlessly to use his strength of both body and soul to satisfy the requirements of the law, to extinguish covetousness through mortification of the flesh, and to stifle natural pride under the weight of voluntary penances and humiliations? Because in him God is preparing one who is to reform the church. His long years of legal righteousness will make him ⸺ ⸺ ⸺ or the delights of the gospel's liberty. Shaking off at last the unbearable yoke from his weary shoulders, he will teach the world to value the pure gospel just by the accent with which he pronounces the words *faith, grace, Word of God*. These words will seem to have been raised from the tomb when they leave the lips of this fortunate refugee from the works of the law and the word of men.

It is the lectern of Wittenberg and the friary of Erfurt that made Luther and his reform. It is also the school of Gamaliel and the rigors of the Pharisees that made Saul of Tarsus and his apostleship.

THE VOICE OF EXPERIENCE

Someone has to stand up to the Jewish doctors, who are bristling with schoolroom nuances, gifted at denaturing a text under the guise of explaining it, "straining out a gnat and swallowing a camel!" (Matthew 23:24), and crediting the most foolish human imaginings to God. Who can accomplish this better than the Jewish doctor who has spent so many years versed in their fallacious arguments and their forced interpretations? He can battle against them with their own weapons and will know how to present to them, according to their desire, either the ingenious and subtle proofs to which they have long been accustomed or the simple and solid reasons that dawn on every mind that is disposed to the truth.

Yet, above all (for this is the main point), someone has to prove the error of the legal righteousness from which the Pharisee seeks peace—a peace that either escapes him or seduces him. Someone has to show the world that nothing justifies, nothing sanctifies, nothing consoles a poor sinner except the totally free grace of God in "Jesus Christ and him crucified" (1 Corinthians 2:2).[3] Who can accomplish this task

---

[3] See also Romans 3:24. [A.M.]

better than the young Pharisee who began with a personal and painful apprenticeship to the very law whose impotence he is to reveal to the world (see Romans 8:3)? He found neither rest for his soul nor strength against sin until the day he believed in the grace to which he had long been an ardent and sincere adversary.

Having penetrated more deeply than Moses into Moses' words, "He [Abraham] believed the LORD, and he counted it to him as righteousness" (Genesis 15:6), and having penetrated more deeply than Habakkuk into Habakkuk's words, "The righteous shall live by his faith" (Habakkuk 2:4), Paul can also say with David—and with a greater depth of feeling than David—"I believed, therefore have I spoken" (Psalm 116:10 KJV).

THE EXAMPLE OF ROMANS

Therein lies—to cite just one example, but an example that encompasses all the others—therein lies the living and fertile source from which the Epistle to the Romans emerged. I have said before and I repeat: In the inspiration of the Scriptures, it is God's Spirit who speaks, but it is also man's spirit. God's Spirit speaks with all his authority, but man's spirit speaks with all his experiences, all his battles, all his sorrows. This is doubly true for the inspiration of the New Testament, freer and more personal than that of the Old because it is more spiritual. Just as it is true to say that the hand of the apostle Paul was directed by God's Spirit in writing the Epistle to the Romans, it is just as true to say that the hand of the apostle Paul drew largely from the heart of Saul of Tarsus in writing the Epistle to the Romans.

Consider the apostle Paul as he gives this striking testimony to the grace of God: "For by works of the law no human being will be justified in his sight. . . . But now the righteousness of God has been manifested apart from the law, although the Law and the Prophets bear witness to it—the righteousness of God through faith in Jesus Christ for all who believe . . . and are justified by his grace as a gift, through the redemption that is in Christ Jesus" (Romans 3:20–22, 24). There, within Paul, you can discern the former Saul of Tarsus working in order to please God, but working "not according to knowledge" (Romans 10:2). He was without success because, seeking to establish his own righteousness, he did not submit to God's righteousness (Romans 10:3).

Consider the apostle Paul, filled with this abundant consolation: "Therefore, since we have been justified by faith, we have peace with God through our Lord Jesus Christ. Through him we have also obtained access by faith into this grace in which we stand, and we rejoice in hope of the glory of God. More than that, we rejoice in our sufferings" (Romans 5:1–3). There, within Paul, you can discern the former Saul of Tarsus pursuing peace without ever attaining it, because he asked it from obedience to the law instead of from the freedom of grace.

Consider the apostle Paul discovering some strange power of sin working in God's holy law for whoever expects righteousness and life from it: "But sin, seizing an opportunity through the commandment, produced in me all kinds of covetousness. Apart from the law, sin lies dead. I was once alive apart from the law, but when the commandment came, sin came alive and I died. The very commandment that promised life proved to be death to me" (Romans 7:8–10).[4] There, within Paul, you can discern the former Saul of Tarsus struggling with that terrible law and garnering from this imprudent struggle only the fruit of finding sin to be more alive, more tyrannical, and at the same time more accursed within him than ever before.

---

[4] See also 1 Corinthians 15:56 and Galatians 3:21. [A.M.]

Finally consider the apostle Paul, breaking into songs of triumph, as if he can no longer contain the thanksgiving welling up from his soul: "Who shall separate us from the love of Christ? Shall tribulation, or distress, or persecution, or famine, or nakedness, or danger, or sword? . . . No, in all these things we are more than conquerors through him who loved us. For I am sure that neither death nor life, nor angels nor rulers, nor things present nor things to come, nor powers, nor height nor depth, nor anything else in all creation, will be able to separate us from the love of God in Christ Jesus our Lord" (Roman 8:35, 37–39). There, within Paul, you can discern the former Saul of Tarsus defeated, exhausted, out of breath, giving way under the weight of a burden he could not bear yet dared not set down, and ready, in the end, to doubt both God and himself.

In summary, Paul would never have been able to write the Epistle to the Romans without the experiences of Saul any more than he could have written it without the light of God's Spirit. It is the same with everything else in his ministry. Paul would never have become Paul if he hadn't begun by being Saul. Saul's weakness is Paul's strength.[5]

WEAKNESS TO STRENGTH

What about you, my dear brother? You have mental weaknesses that weigh on you more than all the others. Perhaps it is an old spirit of discouragement and melancholy that cuts the vigor out of your persevering acts. Perhaps it is many a prejudice based on birth or education from which you don't know how to free a faith that is not yet well grounded, having been acquired late in life. Perhaps it is a long slavery to habits, relationships, or customs that are out

---

[5] Similarly, the apostle is everywhere pleased to recall what he had previously been. (See Acts 22 and 26, 1 Timothy 1:13–16, etc.). [A.M.]

of accord with the requirements of the Christian life. Perhaps it is. . . Or is it all of that and other things besides?

Very well, my dear Saul of Tarsus, there you are in a good school for becoming an apostle Paul. Give yourself no rest until you have found a way to change each of these weaknesses into a strength. Tell yourself firmly that there is no mistake, no prejudice, no bad habit, no mental infirmity, whatever it might be, that, once recognized, cannot in its own way enter into God's plan and make you more fit to serve him today than you could have been without its help. "When I am weak, then I am strong."

HIS PHYSICAL WEAKNESS

If mental weaknesses are the deepest, *physical weaknesses* are the most keenly felt and, if I may say so, the closest to us. Nor was our apostle spared from them.

AN APPEARANCE OF STRENGTH

When we look at Saint Paul in the Acts of the Apostles or in his letters, we see all the voyages he made, crossing the Roman Empire from one end to the other in every direction. We see the gigantic labor he accomplished in his preaching, in the churches he founded, in his correspondence, watches, and prayers. Thus, unless we have thought carefully about it, we will catch ourselves attributing to him an uncommon physical strength, a vigorous constitution, a temperament immune to every fatigue.

This thought is completely natural. It served to guide the ordinary artists who have tried to depict our apostle. Big, handsome, imposing, ideal, a bit like a demigod of paganism—this is how Saint Paul appears in their statues and paintings. But we know that Raphael painted him differently.

He understood that the highest point of genius is to harmonize the needs of art with the data of history. In painting Saint Paul he was inspired by the portrait Saint Paul gives of himself in the second epistle to the Corinthians.

This epistle is so very precious because of the hints that it opens up to us about the person and character of the apostle. I say the "hints," because Saint Paul is careful not to dwell on these matters; he has better things to do than talk about himself. We are reduced to catching his thoughts in a few fleeting remarks.

I won't get into the ingenious discussions that have been raised as to the nature of Saint Paul's physical infirmities, but I am not afraid to state that they were great and seemed to present an obstacle to his ministry. I say this, above all, because of two indications given in our epistle.

Two Hints of Physical Weakness

One such indication is found even in my text: "A thorn was given me in the flesh, a messenger of Satan to harass me, to keep me from being too elated. Three times I pleaded with the Lord about this, that it should leave me. [6] But he said to me, 'My grace is sufficient for you, for my power is made perfect in weakness'" (2 Corinthians 12:7–9).

People have tried in vain to make that thorn a spiritual thorn—that is to say, some extraordinary temptation that the apostle would have despaired of conquering—but this is a man who was given to the world to tell it and to show it that the believer "can do all things through him [Christ] who strengthens" him (Philippians 4:13) and that there is no such thing as invincible temptation any more than there

---

[6] As I see it, the thorn was given not by the messenger of Satan but by the Lord, whom the apostle asks to withdraw it from his servant. See Job 7:16, 14:6; Psalm 39:14 (explained by v. 11). [A.M.]

is inevitable sin. Therefore let us take these words in their natural sense. "A thorn in the flesh" is not a thorn in the spirit.

Please don't argue that the thorn is attributed to Satan's influence, for in 1 Corinthians 5:5 Saint Paul recognizes— and here he is only following his Master (see Luke 13:16)— that Satan has a large part even in the physical ills of humanity.[7]

If any doubt could remain on his thought, it will be removed by the second indication in our epistle. "They say, 'His letters are weighty and strong, but his bodily presence is weak, and his speech of no account'" (2 Corinthians 10:10).[8] Even given the prejudice against the apostle's ministry on the part of the men to whom he ascribes this language, we can believe them as to the weakness of his body, since they have no difficulty giving justice to the strength of his letters. It is possible they may have exaggerated the weakness, but all exaggeration supposes a reality which serves as its support.

Moreover, the apostle, in his response, implicitly agrees with the truth of their report. "Let such a person understand that what we say by letter when absent, we do when present" (2 Corinthians 10:11). He doesn't deny the infirmity that is attributed to his bodily presence; he only claims that he will make up for it, and then some, through vigorous action.

THE MAGNITUDE OF HIS WEAKNESS

After that, there can be no doubt that Saint Paul had a weak body. This weakness was noticeable enough to others that it could be cited as a well-known fact and was of such a

---

[7] Monod's thought here is that Satan's influence does not preclude Paul's physical weakness, his "thorn in the flesh," from being part of his inherent nature and of God's plan for him.

[8] See also 10:1. [A.M.]

nature as to undermine his ministry through its shocking contrast with the power of his letters. As for himself, this weakness was sufficiently painful, humiliating and prejudicial to his work, that Paul had great difficulty resigning himself to it and prayed three times to be freed from it. Three times! This would be nothing for us, but it was a lot for him. To ask for a grace without receiving it was something unheard of in the history of his prayers. What granted prayer could say more to us about their power than this rejected prayer says through the amazement it gave him?

How did this infirmity that I'm considering come on Saint Paul? Was it from birth or through an accident? Was it through self-imposed mortifications and penances during the blind days of his self-righteousness? Was it through the weariness and persecutions that he had suffered and that were enough to ruin the most robust health (see 2 Corinthians 11:23–29)? We don't know. Each of these causes may have contributed. Whatever the case—and this is all we need to know—this giant of an apostle, this spiritual conqueror of half of Asia and all of Europe, had a bodily weakness that was visibly striking, that emboldened his adversaries, that troubled him, and that seemed to make him forever unsuited to his work.

STRENGTH OUT OF WEAKNESS

Very well, in God's eyes, it served only to make him more suited to his work. Or rather, God had thus weakened him for the express purpose of being able to glorify himself without hindrance. We saw him do this earlier in reducing Gideon's army—winnowing after winnowing—to such a small band that he could, at last, give it the victory without fear of it being explained by the number of victors (Judges 7:2, 4, 7). With Paul, if he had had a healthier body and a more vigorous constitution, he would not have trembled as he trembled, despaired of himself as he so despaired, or cried out to God as he cried out. As a result, he would not have done what he did. "Therefore I will boast all the more gladly of my weaknesses, so that the power of Christ may rest upon me" (2 Corinthian 12:9).

This experience is not unique to Saint Paul. Many of the men who have accomplished the greatest things in the world—above all, those who have labored for the Lord and for his kingdom—have had weak constitutions. Saint Bernard was weak, so that one can scarcely comprehend how he found the time and energy for such vast and varied works. Calvin was weak; he died at age 53 after having battled, day after day, against painful infirmities and cruel suffering. Luther himself was far from having the robust health often attributed to him.[9]

Contemporary history gives us other examples, which each of us will find in his own recollections. There are the weak, high strung, sickly women who seem to do little more than exchange one illness for another and have only a breath of life in them. Yet some of them have exhibited lives that are among the fullest and most useful ever displayed on earth.

Nature may well claim its part in the explanation of this astounding phenomenon. We know that a weaker constitution is often linked to a more agile temperament, and it is not without good reason that certain words, such as *tender* or *delicate*, denote both bodily weakness and strength of mind and spirit.[10] However, this is of only secondary importance when it comes to the things of God. The true explanation is

---

[9] Adolphe Monod, too, battled frequent health problems all through the years of his ministry and died at age 54 after a period of great suffering from liver cancer.

[10] Here "mind and spirit" translate the French word *esprit*. It is most often used to mean "mind" but is also, especially in religious contexts, used for "spirit," and both seem appropriate here.

the moral explanation, the providential explanation, Saint Paul's explanation.

FINDING THAT STRENGTH

Listen, then, all of you, the sickly and downhearted family of God's people. Your minds have a holy ambition but are sadly imprisoned in the bonds of the flesh. Your desires reach out for heaven but are tied to the dust through your physical organs. You burn to expend all your energy for the glory of God and the good of humanity, but you cast a discouraged glance on your feeble body, its frail members, its uncertain health, on the whole languishing "outer nature" (2 Corinthians 4:16). Do not let yourself be beaten down. Lift up, "lift your drooping hands and strengthen your weak knees" (Hebrews 12:12). Dream no more except of giving yourself strength from your weakness, just as Saint Bernard, as Calvin, as Luther, and as the apostle Paul did.

You can do it; one can always do it. Yes, by redoubling your faith and prayers, you can gain greater aptitude for your work than you would have had with the strength that you lack and the health for which you long. "When I am weak, then I am strong."

HIS WEAKNESS OF SPEECH

One last weakness remains. It is more formidable than the others for the apostleship of Saint Paul. Dare I name it? It is a *weakness of speech*.

A SPECIAL WEAKNESS

Among the varied weaknesses that threaten to compromise an enterprise, there is often one particular weakness that strikes so directly at its heart that it seems it must infallibly prove fatal. This is what poor vision would be for a painter, or poor hearing for a musician. And this is what poor speech would be for an apostle, because the work entrusted to an apostle is essentially a work of speech. Traveling, organizing, even writing are only the accessories of apostleship; speaking is its substance, its soul, its life.

In addition, one can scarcely recall the success Saint Paul obtained without crediting him with everything that makes up an accomplished orator: a resonant voice, easy diction, pleasing language, a noble and expressive gesture. And yet, one would be fooling himself in imagining Saint Paul endowed with all those advantages. Apollos, yes. Saint Augustine, yes. Théodore de Bèze, yes. Jacques Saurin, yes.[11] But Saint Paul, no.

I hasten to explain myself. Far be it from me to refuse Saint Paul all the natural gifts of eloquence. We cannot doubt that he had many of them, that he had the loveliest of them—clarity of thought, forcefulness of idea, strong emotion, choice of expression, warmth and liveliness of language. I repeat what Neander said: "He would have had no cause to yield to any of the masters of thought or speech of whom ancient Greece could boast."

Yet Saint Paul must have lacked certain external gifts, which are of only secondary importance for the reflective person but which make up the glory and prize of speaking in the eyes of the ordinary person—the gifts of strength, voice quality, action, sparkle.[12] Paul was a man of great eloquence in the most elevated sense of the term, but Paul was not a

---

[11] Théodore de Bèze (1519-1605) was Calvin's successor in Geneva, and Jacques Saurin (1677-1730) was a Huguenot pastor, well known for his eloquence.

[12] This in no way contradicts Acts 14:12, which says that in Lystra Paul was regarded as the chief speaker. [A.M.]

great orator in the popular meaning of this title. I find the
proof of this in the same epistle and even in the same passages that just enabled us to glimpse his physical weakness.
This suggests that the apostle's physical weakness was the
main cause, perhaps the only cause, of his oratorical weakness. . . and you need to grant me this terminology, whose
preciseness you are about to see.

PROOFS OF THIS WEAKNESS

You have heard what certain people said of Paul, "His
letters are weighty and strong, but his bodily presence is
weak, and his speech of no account" (2 Corinthians 10:10).
Think about it. This is talking about Saint Paul, though one
can scarcely persuade himself of the fact. One more time,
please don't tell me, "This is an enemy speaking; this can't be
trusted." Those who held to these hardly-benevolent statements were, perhaps, less enemies than they were ill-disposed
listeners, but I won't insist on that remark. Let them be
enemies, if you want, but even an enemy would not tell those
who have heard a great orator, "His speech is of no account." For Saint Paul's enemies to be able to characterize
his speech as of no account while also treating his bodily
presence as weak, his bodily weakness must have dragged
some oratorical weakness along with it, though I will inten-
tionally refrain from speculating on its exact nature.

Beyond that, Saint Paul does not defend himself against
this reproach in his reply, which I have already quoted.
Instead, by calling only on the power he has "in action," he
implicitly acknowledges that he is lacking "in speech." He
even acknowledges it explicitly in the next chapter, in a verse
that, I confess, sounds quite strange when one reads it for the
first time. "Even if I am unskilled in speaking, I am not so in
knowledge" (2 Corinthians 11:6). To this you can add the
testimony of his first epistle: "And I, when I came to you,

brothers, did not come proclaiming to you the testimony of God with lofty speech or wisdom. . . . And I was with you in weakness and in fear and much trembling, and my speech and my message were not in plausible words of wisdom, but in demonstration of the Spirit and of power, that your faith might not rest in the wisdom of men but in the power of God" (1 Corinthians 2:1, 3–5).

AN UNEXPECTED WEAKNESS

All this reveals an ensemble of weaknesses that would most likely have confused us if we had seen him with our own eyes. When we have just met someone for the first time, having only known him through his writings or his works, we are sometimes quite surprised to find him so different from what we have imagined him to be, but I don't think there has ever been a man who would have excited this sort of surprise by his appearance more keenly than Saint Paul. In spite of all the reflections we just made, if someone had shown him to us in some corner of Corinth or Athens or Rome, we ourselves would scarcely have believed our eyes. "What!" we might have said, "This man, so small in appearance, so fearful and so trembling; this man with a sickly body, ordinary language, and speech that is of no account; this man who drags around a painful thorn lodged in his flesh—this is Saint Paul, this is the apostle of apostles?" Yes, that is he, and all the more so for having been seen by you as so weak and so puny.

THE VALUE OF WEAKNESS

Weakness of speech can have its own kind of strength, even in the eyes of man, because it reveals the moral value of the speech, which is its true power. For example, who does not know how many times the speech of a child is effective where that of a mature man would only have failed? How many times have the last exhortations of a dying man—slow, slurred, scarcely intelligible—stirred a heart more than the firmest, most eloquent discourse could have done?

But let's leave this kind of consideration aside in order to see only what this weakness of speech accomplishes in God's eyes. When one knows himself to be weak, he is left with no other resource than God's strength, grasped by faith and substituted for the human strength he lacks.

If you stripped Paul of his weakness, deprived him of his thorn in the flesh (whatever it might be), and provided him with the good voice, tall stature, and oratorical power that you would claim for him, he would have been able to take his place among the Chrysostoms or Whitefields—those men whom hundreds of souls will hail on the last day as their spiritual fathers because they placed the lovely gifts with which nature endowed them at the service of Jesus Christ. Yet Paul would not have been Saint Paul; he would have been incapable of it through too much ability. A hidden seed of complacency and self-confidence might have remained within the recesses of his heart—a seed that perhaps could never be completely uprooted.

Yet such as we just saw Paul and with the task that he had before him, he had only one pathway to take, and he took it. He threw himself without reserve into the Lord's arms. The orator disappears into his discourses, just as the man disappears into his life. The one who said, "It is no longer I who live, but Christ who lives in me" (Galatians 2:20) is also the one who could have said in the extremity to which his weakness of speech reduced him, "It is no longer I who speak, but God who speaks in me."

MOSES AND PAUL

Thus Saint Paul repeated Moses' experience. By being "slow of speech" (Exodus 4:10), Moses was reduced to being "as God" who reveals, while leaving to his brother Aaron the role of the "mouth" (Exodus 4:16) that transmits those revelations (see also Numbers 12:3). Thus Moses was made "mighty in his words" through the infirmity of his speech, just as he was made "mighty in his . . . deeds" through his weakness of character (Acts 7:22).

This double marvel should never be forgotten. Moses was, without contradiction, the greatest instrument of the Spirit of God in the Old Testament, just as Saint Paul was, without contradiction, his greatest instrument in the New Testament. Neither of them had powerful speech. This is all the more significant in that each had an orator beside him. Moses had Aaron, who could "speak well" (Exodus 4:14), and Paul had Apollos, "an eloquent man" (Acts 18:24). Strength makes an Aaron, but weakness alone makes a Moses. Strength makes an Apollos, but weakness alone makes a Saint Paul.

YOUR SPECIAL WEAKNESS

After all this, dare you complain that you have been refused the special strength you need for your work? Dare you complain that you have a great household to direct without having a spirit of organization? Or that you have serious and complicated business to pursue without having a spirit of perseverance? Or that you have to speak or to write without having the gift of speech or of pen? Unbelieving as you are, let go of these debilitating calculations.

Is the work you are considering truly your work, the work God has assigned to you as your very own? Is it your work, just as guiding Israel through the desert was Moses' work and evangelizing the Gentiles was Saint Paul's work? That is the question to resolve through reflection, prayer, and every other means at your disposal—unless it is fully resolved by a clear obligation. There is no need of reflection or prayer, for example, to assure the father of a family that it is his mission to raise his children, or to assure a servant that it is his mission to maintain order in the house of his masters.

Once this question is resolved and your work has been well determined, go fearlessly forward! God who calls you is also saying to you, as he said to Gideon—whether to the ear of the body or the ear of the spirit matters little—"Go in this might of yours; . . . do not I send you?" (Judges 6:14). This special weakness from which you could not be delivered remains so that you might make a special strength of it through faith. Resign yourself to be a Moses, since you cannot be an Aaron; resign yourself to be a Saint Paul, since you cannot be an Apollos.

What a doctrine, oh my God! Who can believe it? Even those who preach it, do they really believe it? "If you know these things, blessed are you if you do them" (John 13:17). Yes, "when I am weak, then I am strong."

FEARLESSLY FORWARD

Saul of Tarsus, such as he was, was chosen by God to become the apostle Paul through a preparation of weakness—a preparation of which his career would offer many other examples, and which, in addition to the services it had already rendered, finally adds that of revealing to him, both for his sake and for ours, the profound truth of my text: "When I am weak, then I am strong."

Very well then, you Christians who have it on your hearts not to traverse this earth without accomplishing your work but whose work overwhelms your weakness, take Saint Paul's motto today as your own: "When I am weak, then I am strong." Apply it to yourselves without further delay for fear that, according to the sobering words of one of God's servants, "you might come to die before you have begun to live."

SUCH AS I AM

Such as I am—not such as I was yesterday, or such as I will be tomorrow, but such as I am today.

Such as I am, if my heart is right before God, if I have resolved to accomplish his work whatever the cost. Here I am, prepared by a preparation that is worth all the preparations I regret not having had.

Such as I am, "Behold, I have come to do your will, O God" (Hebrews 10:7).

Such as I am and whatever I must become, even if I am only a poor Saul of Tarsus and must become an apostle Paul!

Oh my God, do not leave within me a single weakness that you do not convert into strength, a single sorrow that you do not change into joy, a single temptation that you do not turn into victory, a single void that you do not fill with yourself!

A CHARGE TO THE YOUNG

You young people who are listening to me, I began with you, and it is with you that I would end. For you, everything is serious: your age because it is the start of your careers, and the times in which we live because they are filled with storms. And may I add before God, who searches hearts, that your hearts are serious too?

Do you desire to do the work God has confided to you on earth, whatever might come of it and whatever might be said of it? Very well then, start today by committing yourself to his service, rich with all that you have and enriched still more by all that you lack. The one who had just multiplied the loaves and who can equally multiply every kind of resource you possess said, "Gather up the leftover fragments, that nothing may be lost" (John 6:12).

Therefore, gather up everything you have by way of strength—health, vigor, enthusiasm, natural ability, acquired light—and carry it all to Jesus Christ. Keep none of it for yourselves. Do you not belong completely to him? And do you not belong all the more to yourselves for having given yourselves completely to him?

Also gather up, above all gather up everything you have by way of weakness—your physical infirmity, your ignorance, your inexperience, your slowness to understand, your difficulty in learning, everything that beats you down and discourages you—and carry it to him so that he can turn it into strength from God, better than all your own strength.

Strong in your weakness and such as you are, my young friends, by faith!

BY FAITH

What made Paul out of Saul? Faith. Who else has put what is written in the eleventh chapter of the Epistle to the Hebrews into practice the way he did?

By faith Saul of Tarsus, making his way toward Damascus, exchanged the path of persecution for that of the martyr. By faith Saul filled the known world with the name of Jesus Christ and did a work that no other human work has ever equaled, either in breadth or in depth. By faith Saul, triumphing over a rebellious nature, achieved a level of Christian life that would have been judged above what is possible for man, if it hadn't been lived out in his story.

"Go, and do likewise" (Luke 10:37). It is not a question of strength; it is a question of faith.

✽

❖ *fifth discourse* ❖

HIS POWERFUL EXAMPLE

_____

HIS POWERFUL EXAMPLE

Philippians 3:4–17

If anyone else thinks he has reason for confidence in the flesh, I have more: circumcised on the eighth day, of the people of Israel, of the tribe of Benjamin, a Hebrew of Hebrews; as to the law, a Pharisee; as to zeal, a persecutor of the church; as to righteousness, under the law blameless. But whatever gain I had, I counted as loss for the sake of Christ. Indeed, I count everything as loss because of the surpassing worth of knowing Christ Jesus my Lord. For his sake I have suffered the loss of all things and count them as rubbish, in order that I may gain Christ and be found in him, not having a righteousness of my own that comes from the law, but that which comes through faith in Christ, the righteousness from God that depends on faith—that I may know him and the power of his resurrection, and may share his sufferings, becoming like him in his death, that by any means possible I may attain the resurrection from the dead.

Not that I have already obtained this or am already perfect, but I press on to make it my own, because Christ Jesus has made me his own. Brothers, I do not consider that I have made it my own. But one thing I do: forgetting what lies behind and straining forward to what lies ahead, I press on toward the goal for the prize of the upward call of God in Christ Jesus. Let those of us who are mature think this way, and if in anything you think otherwise, God will reveal that also to you. Only let us hold true to what we have attained.

Brothers, JOIN IN IMITATING ME, and keep your eyes on those who walk according to the example you have in us.

AN EXAMPLE TO FOLLOW

"Join in imitating me." There is the goal to which all these discourses were intended to lead. Let us repeat one more time: in talking to you about Paul, I have had no desire to glorify Paul. My desire has been to offer you an example, so that those who have it on their hearts to be conformed to God's will and to accomplish their work might model themselves on it. We have the perfect example in Jesus Christ and in him alone, but God has accommodated himself to a need of our weakness in also showing us imperfect examples. These, while remaining well behind the Master, walk well ahead of us. Their natural infirmity, while not destroyed, has been so well contained that it has left the way open for a true, complete, and victorious Christian life. Paul is one of these imperfect examples, and perhaps the least imperfect that has ever been given on earth.

"IMITATE ME"

If a final proof should be required of me, after all those that we have seen, I would find it in the exhortation of my text: "Join in imitating me." This is a familiar exhortation in the mouth of our apostle; he addressed it, in turn, to the Philippians (4:9), the Thessalonians (1 Thessalonians 1:6, 2 Thessalonians 3:6–8), the Corinthians (1 Corinthians 4:16, 11:1), and all the churches (see Acts 20:35, etc.).

Try to imagine the most exemplary Christian you have ever known saying to anyone, "Imitate me." There are only two ways to explain such language. Either it is the most prideful blindness about oneself (and I leave it to you to think whether such an explanation is appropriate for the apostle Paul), or it represents a holiness so great and yet so simple that it rises as far above the precautions of modesty as it does above the pretensions of self-love, so as to give glory to God's grace alone.

Do you not think, as I do, that someone who could say "Join in imitating me" must have had a Christian life that was not just more faithful than that of the least unfaithful among us but totally different from it? Do you share the feelings that Saint Paul inspires in me and that have only grown with the new study I just made of his life? Are you pierced with respect, gratitude, and love for the apostle to the Gentiles?

If so, then I rejoice, but only on one condition. Don't rest there. I want you to seek for yourselves what you praise in him. I don't want you to evade the duty of imitation through the pleasure of admiration. Finally, I don't want you complacently to substitute the prideful and sterile "Admire me" for that pressing, fertile, and dangerous lesson of the holy apostle, "Imitate me."

THE COST OF DISCIPLESHIP

Yes, dangerous. I am being careful not to take you by surprise. Our Master, far from hiding from his disciples the cost of following him, seemed to take on the task of revealing it. Through the paradoxical force of his language, he disclosed the sacrifices he was demanding of those who were his. "If anyone comes to me and does not hate his own father and mother and wife and children and brothers and sisters, yes, and even his own life, he cannot be my disciple. Whoever does not bear his own cross and come after me cannot be my disciple. . . . So therefore, any one of you who does not renounce all that he has cannot be my disciple" (Luke 14:26–27, 33). As the servant of this Master, I want to use the same honesty with you that he used with them.

Beyond that, this pathway of renouncement that I am openly proposing has a kind of secret attraction for faithful disciples. It only turns aside the doubtful ones, who would distance themselves sooner or later and whose participation would be less a support than an embarrassment for the true people of Jesus Christ.

If then you are preoccupied with "earthly things" (John 3:12)—earthly glory, earthly wealth, earthly contentment, or even earthly affections—watch out for Paul's example and the application I want to draw from it. In hearing me speak of imitating him, there is good reason for you to sense within you something like an invisible hand stretching itself out to protect your money, your well-being, your human glory, your idolatrous attachments. This motion has the rapidity of instinct, but it is also smart. You would risk all this treasure of self-will in enlisting yourself to follow in Paul's footsteps. He made the sacrifice that was asked of him, and it might be asked of you too. It is that much more likely to be asked, because it would cost you more[1].

What if Jesus Christ were to require you to exchange the general favor you enjoy for the humiliations of his life and the disgrace of his death? What if he were to require you to exchange the riches that abound in your homes for the abasement and destitution of poverty—are you listening; of poverty? Or to exchange your comfortable life, dainty food, and immediately-satisfied desires for privations, anxieties, sufferings of the body, and torments of the spirit? Or to exchange the sweet company of loved ones who are the pleasure of your eyes and the joy of your heart for separation, heartbreak, and bitter solitude? Or. . .

Do you feel within yourself that you are ready to "suffer the loss of all things . . . in order that you may gain Christ" (see Philippians 3:8)? If you respond with Saint Peter, "Lord, I am ready to go with you both to prison and to death" (Luke 22:33), all that remains is to probe deep inside yourself and be sure that you are under no illusions. But if you respond inwardly, "This is a hard saying; who can listen to it?" (John 6:60), everything has been said. Here I am not considering whether you can save your soul, such as you are, but for sure, such as you are, you cannot be an imitator of Saint Paul.

THOSE WHO REFUSE

Moreover, if you refuse to imitate him, you will find yourself in very numerous and, alas, very Christian company. Saint Paul warns you of that himself, but he sees in this only one more reason to urge you to follow his example—an example which is all the more precious for being so rare. "Keep your eyes on those who walk according to the example you have in us. For many, of whom I have often told you and

---

[1] See Matthew 19:21. [A.M.]

now tell you even with tears, walk as enemies of the cross of Christ. Their end is destruction, their god is their belly, and they glory in their shame, with minds set on earthly things" (Philippians 3:17–19).

Concerning their number, there are many like that, and concerning their nature, they are Christians, not pagans, or else the apostle would be less astonished at their sins and less fearful of the seduction of their example. I will go further. They are Christians whom, by all appearances, the church has not barred from communion, their unfaithfulness being of such a nature that it offers nothing for human discipline to lay hold of.

It is true that "their God is their belly," and that "they glory in their shame," but these harsh accusations should be interpreted from the point of view of Scripture, which shows holy severity toward things that escape the world's censure and even the church's rule. The apostle's true thought is revealed in the last trait, which completes and sums up his sad depiction: "With minds set on earthly things." This trait does not apply only to men given over to shameful unruliness of the flesh. It applies equally to those Christians who are irreproachable before the law of the world, unassailable before that of the church, and whose total crime is the preeminence they grant to material interests, even though their "citizenship is in heaven" (Philippians 3:20).[2]

If the apostle treats them as "enemies of the cross of Christ," that does not imply they are opposed to the doctrine of the cross. He is not complaining about their doctrine, but about their life. They are enemies of the cross because they reject a crucified existence. In that sense, one can be an enemy of the cross and very orthodox; one can be an enemy of the cross and zealous for the spread of the gospel; one can be

[2] Further descriptions of such Christians are given in Romans 16:18, Titus 1:11–12, etc. [A.M.]

an enemy of the cross and an active, influential member of the best religious institutions; one can be an enemy of the cross and preach the cross with fervor and eloquence.

There is a comparison here that both strikes and terrifies me. If there are enemies of the cross in the little church of Philippi—fully alive, fully apostolic, fully disciplined as it was—how many will there be in our large, fallen, and languishing church, which lacks the former orderliness and where everyone lives according to what pleases him![3] How many perhaps even among those who have known the truth, professed it, defended it! Ah, to escape the cross of Christ and the example of Saint Paul, you only have to live like the majority of Christians, believing Christians, Christians who are honored in the world and noted in the church.

PREPARED HEARTS

Yet in the end, "many" is not "all." I know that there are today, here and elsewhere, in this communion and in others, quite a few Christians who desire at any cost to be imitators of Paul, just as he was of Jesus Christ. They sigh after a true Christian life, recognizing that until now they have lacked it. They understand that they can no longer find rest for themselves except in following their light to the very end, in taking the gospel completely seriously, and in having their wills conformed, submitted, and sacrificed without reservation to the will of God.

I said that I know it. I will go further: I sense it. Yes, I sense it even in this very moment, through that mysterious sympathy that is established in a large assembly between the one who speaks and those who listen. I sense that my language finds an echo in more than one heart. I sense, I tell you, that more than one heart burns, as does mine, at the

---

[3] See Judges 17:6 [A.M.]

very mention of this Christian life that should be so well known and is so little known.

Beyond that, this is not a localized or passing impression, and I am happy to give this testimony to our Christian generation, which I am not accustomed to flattering. I don't believe I have seen this need, this "hunger and thirst for righteousness," experienced in any period of our present-day religious history more deeply or more generally than it is today. I hear on every side that the religious awakening has declined, yet for my part, I like to think that this decline is more apparent than real. I grant that there is, perhaps, less fervor than previously, less diligence in the disciplines, less enthusiasm for works, less firmness of doctrine—I should say, perhaps, in the conception of doctrine. And you can believe it costs me dearly to grant all this. Yet there is no less "hunger and thirst for righteousness," and I even believe there is more. This is what reassures me, because this is the essential point. Is it not written, "Blessed are those who hunger and thirst for righteousness, for they shall be satisfied" (Matthew 5:6)?

DAYS OF CRISIS; DAYS OF RENEWAL

What is happening today to the awakening is what sometimes happens to the believer. After the happy years of first love—where prayer is frequent, work is sweet, life is easy, heaven is serene, and earth is fertile—many a soul experiences a season of darkness, apathy, and growing cold. He is disappointed in more than one godly expectation, finds himself engaged again in more than one battle he thought he had vanquished forever, and has learned through bitter experience to be distrustful of self. Troubled, disconcerted, and beaten down, the faithful soul begins to ask whether the gospel has really given him all that he was promised. He complains about himself, about others, and—for all I know—about God and his Word. Yet he complains as Job did, without giving up hope (Job 13:15). And like Job, he too will gather the fruit of his faith.

Thus there takes place within this soul an inner, painful, but healthy labor from which you will see him emerge, if you have the patience to wait, blessed by God in the end more than he was at the beginning (Job 42:11–12). He will be less ardent but more serious, less confident but more humble, less satisfied but more sanctified.

It is the same with the awakening. It is in a period of crisis and transition. Sad, distracted, discontented with itself, and uneasy about the future, it is troubled and turning in every direction without finding rest anywhere. It probes its doctrine, and its doctrine has lost its precision; it probes its ethics, and its ethics have lost their rigor; it probes Scripture, and Scripture itself seems to have lost its clarity and authority. Yet this, too, is the result of an inner labor whose final result can benefit the awakening, provided it doesn't resign itself to remain where it is and provided the "hunger and thirst for righteousness" (Matthew 5:6) continue to torment it relentlessly until it has been satisfied by "true righteousness and holiness" (Ephesians 4:24).

Very well, be at peace! This condition is fulfilled by the awakening; witness the groaning that characterizes every facet of it. There is groaning in its prayers, groaning in its undertakings, groaning in its affections, groaning in its joys, groaning in its good works, groaning in its religious gatherings, so different from what they once were. This groaning is a weakness, I grant, but a weakness from which God will cause his people to draw new strength.

EVEN FOR THE PREACHER

Will I say it? The preacher of the gospel knows double the bitterness of this laborious childbirth. He knows it as a

Christian, and he knows it also as a preacher. With silent regret he recalls the days when his spoken words flowed naturally, when his pen ran without hindrance, when the things to say came to him as if by themselves, and when he was headed with firm and decisive steps down a cleanly defined pathway toward a goal that was clearly perceived and consistently pursued. Those days are no more.

Aside from the great questions—I should have said, the great question of life and death—on which a Christian conscience cannot waver, everything else only appears to him as if obscured by clouds. Too often he makes his way, almost groping, through a ceaseless alternation of light, darkness, and twilight. He doesn't always know what needs to be said, because he doesn't always see what needs to be done. The large crowd that assembles on the appointed day to gather the word of truth from his lips doesn't hear the mute prayer of his distressed soul any more than they saw the battles of his wakeful night or the sterile suffering of his labor. They are blind people, cold people—or, rather, people ignorant of what the gospel ministry is for a serious mind in these serious days.

He, on the other hand, standing at the appointed hour, has already begun to stammer the first words of his discourse, still scarcely discerning how he should speak. No matter. Let him look to the God who sends him! Behind those clouds piled up on the horizon, does he not see a hand stretching itself out and seeking his? Let him boldly place his hand in that fatherly hand, and let him walk with courage! Then, along with the prophet, and all faithful people with him, he can say, "But as for me, I will look to the LORD; I will wait for the God of my salvation; my God will hear me. . . . When I fall, I shall rise; when I sit in darkness, the LORD will be a light to me. . . . He will bring me out to the light; I shall look upon his vindication" (Micah 7:7–9)!

STRENGTHENED IN GOD

Whatever the case, the hour has come not to be beaten down but to be strengthened in God. If God has "for a brief moment deserted" his people, it is so that he can, "with great compassion, gather them" (see Isaiah 54:7). This is the hour of Mary Magdalene. Mary Magdalene seeks Jesus' dead body, and cries out in the torment of her soul, "They have taken away my Lord, and I do not know where they have laid him" (John 20:13). Then behold, Jesus Christ is in front of her, not dead but alive. More than alive, he is resurrected, glorified, and preparing to disappear from before her eyes only to come and dwell in her heart. This is a touching image of today's church: days of crisis are days of renewal.

WHAT TO IMITATE

It is to those hungry and thirsty souls that I address our apostle's exhortation, "Join in imitating me." Saint Paul came during days that had more than one similarity with ours, stirred as they were by a movement just as deep, just as formidable as the one we are witnessing. Faced with a pagan world falling into dissolution and a Judaism straying into unfaithful paths, the work God had entrusted to the apostle was the renewing of the Roman Empire through the gospel. The apostle accomplished that work. But what did he do in the process? What would he do today if he were in our place, if God called him to restore a church in decline and a society in peril by restoring the Christian faith? In answering these questions, we are not left to conjecture. Before writing, "Join in imitating me," Paul was careful to say what he wanted them to imitate, and the means by which he himself had become what he was. His entire secret is to glory in Jesus Christ and in him alone.

GLORYING IN CHRIST

This explanation from eighteen hundred years ago applies no less to us and to our needs than if it were taken from contemporary history. A general characteristic of the men whom God inspires is that they speak a timeless message; by this alone one should recognize them as men set apart. While speaking "in an earthly way" (John 3:31), they take part to some extent in the privilege of the One who "is speaking. . . from heaven" (Hebrews 12:25) because he "comes from heaven" (John 3:31). Their word transcends the course of time and traverses the whole evolution of history without losing any of its truth.

Augustine has grown old, because he is filled with things that belong only to his era. For a similar reason, Bernard has also grown old; Calvin and Luther have grown old. Yet Saint Paul, Saint John, Saint Peter have not grown old at all and will never grow old. Each passing generation comes, in its turn, to draw from the inexhaustible treasure of their words, because those words so truly come from a region elevated well above human vicissitudes and because these "men spoke from God as they were carried along by the Holy Spirit" (2 Peter 1:21).

To glory in Jesus Christ and him alone—that was everything for Saint Paul in the first century and it would be everything for him in the nineteenth, for "Jesus Christ is the same yesterday and today and forever" (Hebrews 13:8). Our specific task is not to invent a new Christ, as some seem intent on doing; it is to probe deeper into the knowledge and service of the ancient Christ, ever the same and ever new. He turned Saul into Saint Paul, and he can turn us into his imitators.

AS A CHRISTIAN

Moreover, Saint Paul can more readily offer his example for us to imitate because this example, as he presents it here, is that of a Christian far more than of an apostle. Or rather, it is only that of an apostle because it is that of a Christian. Reread the verses that precede my text, and, I dare say, you will not find a single word that bears the aroma of an apostle. The apostle fades away; only the Christian appears, and the Christian fully in Christ.

I stated elsewhere a thought that is central to the subject at hand, and I willingly return to it here. It is above all through his personal Christianity that Paul is an apostle, and it is through an exceptional Christianity that he is an eminent apostle. One might say that he is only an apostle—that he is only *the* Apostle—through being a Christian.

This is admirable and deeply instructive. There is no appearance of a priestly mindset in Saint Paul. While others, who take themselves for heirs of the apostles, are jealous to separate themselves from the ordinary people of God, Paul shows himself to be just as jealous to identify himself with them.[4] Let those others boast of their clerical nature or their apostolic succession, as if an accusing instinct pressured them to supply outward signs of their vocation in place of the inward signs that are lacking. Paul only glories in what he has in common with the least of God's children. In so doing, he brings out all the more clearly the essential qualifications of his apostleship, which are spiritual. At the same time, he more effectively stimulates us to imitate him, because in putting himself at our level, he increases both our courage and our sense of responsibility. Therefore, do not fear a troublesome glimmer of light;[5] Paul depicts himself without a halo and with traits that nothing prevents you from adopting, whoever you are.

---

[4] See Romans 1:12, 2 Corinthians 12:5–6, etc. [A.M.]
[5] See Exodus 34:35. [A.M.] This refers to the radiance of Moses' skin after he had been in God's presence.

Two Distinctive Traits

These traits—I am speaking only of great traits—can be reduced to two, which in all ages make up the true Christian: his life and the basis of that life, his faith. And these two things are, at their root, only one, so that Saint Paul moves from one to the other, with nothing to indicate a change of subject. The two meet in Jesus Christ. Faith is Jesus Christ in our heart; life is Jesus Christ in our work. Faith is Jesus Christ dying for us; life is Jesus Christ living in us.

Imitating Paul's Life

Here is Saint Paul's *life*, the life we are to strive to make our own: "That I may know him and the power of his resurrection, and may share his sufferings, becoming like him in his death" (Philippians 3:10). The center and soul of this life is in the phrase "becoming like him in his death." If Paul associates himself with "the power of his Master's resurrection," it is through "sharing his sufferings." If he walks toward glory, it is by way of the cross.

The Fellowship of His Suffering

Paul breathes only to suffer. His career, no less precisely than David's, is summed up in the sad words, "My tears have been my food day and night" (Psalm 42:3). This is so true that in a previous discourse we were able to define Paul's Christianity through his tears and use them alone to trace the entire course of his life. He explains himself quite clearly in the rest of our epistle.

He is the disciple of a Master who was "highly exalted" (Philippians 2:9) because he "made himself nothing, . . . becoming obedient to the point of death, even death on a cross" (Philippians 2:7–8). Paul aspires to share Christ's bliss tomorrow by sharing his suffering today, even to the point where death now appears to him as nothing but the desired end of his living martyrdom. "For to me to live is Christ, and to die is gain" (Philippians 1:21).

The Master calls the hour of his sacrifice the hour of his glory. Through a hope filled with sadness and love, he compares himself to a grain of wheat that falls into the earth and can be multiplied only on the condition of its death (John 12:23–24). The disciple is one of those who go through the world "always being given over to death for Jesus' sake, so that the life of Jesus also may be manifested in [their] mortal flesh" (2 Corinthians 4:11).

The Master dies, crucified for his church. The disciple— Oh, boldness! Oh, holy imprudence!—rejoices in his sufferings for the sake of his brothers, and in his flesh he is filling up what is lacking in Christ's afflictions for the sake of his body, that is, the church (Colossians 1:24).

I leave the explanation of this astonishing saying to those who have received grace to penetrate the mysteries of faith, love, and the Christian life. One thing, however, is certain, and it is sufficient for my present purpose: the pen that traced these words was dipped in the experience of a life fully crucified with the crucified Jesus. This life was Saint Paul's, and this life should be yours if you are his imitators.

OUR NEED FOR RENEWAL

Oh, my friends, here is where our Christianity has need, not of gradual growth, but of complete renewal. Where do we see this conformity with the death of Jesus Christ being sought or known or understood among us? Through living in the world and with the world, Christians—true Christians— insensibly let themselves be reassured by its example in the pursuit of self-will, rather than obeying the austere yet sweet voice of the gospel that calls us to glory in the steps of the crucified one.

It is not that these Christians consciously reject the sacrifices of the Christian life. No, I imagine them to be more sincere in their faith than that. Placed squarely between unfaithfulness and impoverishment, between unfaithfulness and suffering, even between unfaithfulness and death, I want to believe, I do believe that they would endure impoverishment, suffering, and death rather than abandon the Lord.

But this terrible choice only presents itself in certain rare and extreme situations. In the ordinary circumstances which make up our everyday life, the cross presents itself in a less formidable and far less precise form, yet a form that is just as real, just as bitter. It is the choice of an entire existence of obedience to God, devotion to our neighbor, and renouncement of self. Yet the flesh shrinks back before this daily crucifying. The cross that we don't want to accept and dare not reject is avoided by turning our gaze aside so as not to be faced with the alternative of either taking it up or fleeing from it. Thus for most of us, the Christian life is translated into a perpetual study to accommodate ourselves to faithful Christianity without "becoming like [Christ] in his death" (Philippians 3:10).

ACCEPTING OUR CROSS

Does this mean I want the Christian to be seeking mortifications of the flesh and penances? Oh, no! That is absolutely not required of him and would even put him at risk of presumption, self-righteousness, and humiliating falls. Why would God be required to strengthen us against temptations that we have voluntarily chosen and rashly dared to take on?

For us as for the Master, it is a matter, not of seeking the cross, but of seeking through the cross for the glory of the resurrection, which is found on no other path. The cross for the sake of the cross, never; but the cross for the Lord's sake, always. The only way to accept the crucified one without the cross is to take the shadow for the reality. Christianity without the cross is Christianity without Christ.

I ask this generation, which is such a friend of well-being and such an enemy of suffering, what have you done with this word from the Master, "Whoever does not bear his own cross and come after me cannot be my disciple" (Luke 14:27)? Your cross! Before bearing it, you have to see it. Show it to me. Where is it? Do you even know that you have one, one that is specifically yours, having been assigned to you by God just as surely as Golgotha's cross was assigned to Jesus Christ?

If one wanted to choose a specific name to characterize this generation's Christianity, he would be tempted to call it *a comfortable Christianity.* If the primitive church, in days of mourning and glory, solved the problem of knowing the measure of suffering that faith can attain without giving way, the church of the nineteenth century seems to have posed the opposite problem of knowing the measure to which faith can be reduced without being denied.

Come, then, martyrs of past centuries, victims of pagan Rome and victims of Christian Rome, all you who have taken the cross too seriously, come and learn from us the secret of serving the Lord without having it cost much at all—just some paltry pleasures on which one would blush to set a price, just a few worldly friendships to which one wasn't very attached, just a little bit of money that death would always end up snatching from us and that is taken neither from the arteries nor from the veins nor from any sensitive part of one's fortune!

AVOIDING EXTREMES

Please bear with the bitterness of my language. Truly, I find myself asking whether the spirit of Saint Paul, the spirit of Jesus Christ, is not still more misunderstood[6] in this pathway than it is in the opposite one of voluntary privations and atoning sufferings. Whatever the case, neither one nor the other of these two extremes is necessary. Imitating Saint Paul will simultaneously preserve us from both.

His example will teach us not to load ourselves with a burden of our own choosing (Colossians 2:20–23); yet this same example will warn us not to draw back from any of the trials God places before us when we desire to "know nothing . . . except Jesus Christ and him crucified" (1 Corinthians 2:2). Therefore, let us walk boldly in his footsteps and leave no room for thinking that error might involve more self-denial than truth, more law than grace, more fear than love.[7] Let us demonstrate the beautiful union between the doctrine richest in promises and the morality most fertile in sacrifices by showing this union realized in us.

Then—I am well aware—we will have our tears, just as the apostle did, but, like him, we will also have our joys, our great joys. Then we will have an answer for those who speak ill of the gospel of grace, whereas today more than one faithful soul feels drawn toward self-righteousness as the opposite of the well-being in which most of God's children are asleep.[8] Then we will be joined together with Jesus Christ

---

[6] The French word *méconnu* here can also be translated as "ignored" or "misjudged."

[7] Monod in this section is arguing for a balanced, Pauline approach to our faith. He has been talking about the problem of falling into "comfortable Christianity." The point here seems to be that in doing so, we indicate to those watching the church that legalism and self-denial are the only errors to avoid. When we follow in Paul's footsteps, we avoid giving this impression.

[8] Here Monod seems to be addressing a false impression that might be given to those in the church (as opposed to outsiders, as above). When they see Christians who have become "conformed to this present age" purporting to be following the gospel of grace, they might feel the need to take the opposite course of self-denial, adopting a legalistic

and we will be his, so that this world, which we have shocked in so many ways, will learn from us what power there is in faith and what disinterestedness there is in a Christian soul. Then. . .

But aren't my words being lost in the air? Are there really many souls here in whom they awaken a like-minded ambition? For all I know, there is some Pharisee here ridiculing me in his heart (Luke 16:14).

One more time, it is not just progress that I ask of you and that I ask of myself. It is a totally new direction. Our Christianity has to be revised!

IMITATING PAUL'S FAITH

A tree is not held upright without roots. The life of renouncement and crucifixion that Saint Paul appropriated for himself—that life so contrary to self-will and to the whole natural man—could not begin in him or be maintained to the end without having been birthed, without being nourished every day by an inner consciousness. This inner consciousness, this source of the life of Jesus Christ in Saint Paul is Saint Paul's faith in Jesus Christ.

BY GRACE

Listen to how the apostle explains himself. "Whatever gain I had, I counted as loss for the sake of Christ. Indeed, I count everything as loss because of the surpassing worth of knowing Christ Jesus my Lord. For his sake I have suffered the loss of all things and count them as rubbish, in order that I may gain Christ and be found in him, not having a righteousness of my own that comes from the law, but that

---

"righteousness." To avoid this, they need to see Christians displaying the kind of balanced Christianity for which Monod is advocating.

which comes through faith in Christ, the righteousness from God that depends on faith" (Philippians 3:7–9). The apostle is so far from seeking any personal expiation, any meritorious virtue, any nourishment of any kind for his self-righteousness that his life of suffering and dying finds its source only in the righteousness from God in Jesus Christ, and that righteousness is applied through faith alone, "in order that the promise may rest on grace" (Romans 4:16).

What a wonderful thing! The most holy and most devoted of men, the one who could most boldly have claimed self-righteousness for himself, if there were self-righteousness (Romans 3:23–24), is the very one who most decisively repudiates all self-righteousness and rests most exclusively on the unique grace of Jesus Christ. This is no coincidence; don't think that it is. There is a deep relationship here. None has been holier and more devoted because none has judged himself to be more freely saved.

Less enlightened minds, less exalted souls in all the Christian communions and in all the world's religions have looked to privation or suffering to provide an imaginary means of appeasing God, of blotting out their sins and deserving heaven. Yet for him, the thing that calls forth and sustains a boundless devotion, both in his heart and in his works, is the unclouded contemplation, the deep awareness of the sacrifice through which Jesus Christ prepared the way for him without his works, before his good works, and in spite of his evil works. The crucified love[9] of the lost creature is a response to the crucified love of the Savior God.

PAUL AND GRACE

Do I need to pile up all the testimonies Saint Paul gives to grace? The easier this task would be, the more superfluous

---

[9] "Crucified love" is love that makes us willing to suffer self-denial for the sake of the loved one.

it is. I rely on whoever has even a superficial knowledge of his discourses and letters, where justification "by grace . . . through faith" (Ephesians 2:8) always occupies first place. It is the central point to which all else is tied. It is more than just one of the apostle's doctrines; it *is* his doctrine. He is an apostle for it alone, just as he became an apostle through it alone. Before it became the object of his entire ministry, it was the basis and soul of his conversion, for the transition from Saul to Paul is nothing but the transition from law to grace.

Paul and grace; grace and Paul; the name and the concept are so inseparable that the one must be looked on as the living personification of the other. Moreover, what point is there in seeking testimony elsewhere when right before our eyes we have language that is as clear, abundant, and firm as that of my text? We only need to reread it. "Whatever gain I had, I counted as loss for the sake of Christ. Indeed, I count everything as loss because of the surpassing worth of knowing Christ Jesus my Lord. For his sake I have suffered the loss of all things and count them as rubbish, in order that I may gain Christ" (Philippians 3:7–8). There is the case he makes for his own works: "loss" and "rubbish." And here is the value he attaches to knowing Jesus Christ: "the surpassing worth of knowing Christ Jesus my Lord."

Do you need a statement more precise and detailed than that? You have it in what follows. "That I may . . . be found in him, not having a righteousness of my own that comes from the law, but that which comes through faith in Christ, the righteousness from God that depends on faith" (Philippians 3:8–9). Such language is so simple and powerful that I would be ashamed—not to mention highly embarrassed—to explain it. Never has a theologian summed up free salvation in fewer words more filled with meaning. Therefore, let no one flatter himself that he can imitate Saint Paul's life without first imitating his faith. He must, as a poor sinner who has fallen "short of the glory of God," abandon himself to "the righteousness of God" alone so as to be "justified by his grace as a gift, through the redemption that is in Christ Jesus" (Romans 3:23–24).

GRACE AND THE AWAKENING

I would not insist so much on this matter if I were speaking fifteen or twenty years ago. In those first days of our religious awakening, days of first light and, alas, of first fervor, this completely free salvation, this justification by faith alone was the ABC of the gospel for whoever had opened his heart to the truth. We who were proclaiming the gospel couldn't find language too expressive to bear witness to it—let us rather say, we couldn't reproduce Saint Paul's language too faithfully—because no language could go too far.

But today, the air is permeated with a kind of hazy theology that goes astray and blushes over the firmness of those beginnings. *Justification by faith* is close to being relegated by some to the ranks of outdated sayings. *Expiation* wounds more than one delicate spirit and no longer dares show itself except veiled in indirect language, lest it offend philosophy. *Grace*, that small word so full and so sweet, that delicious music to a Christian's ear, has lost it charm and comes less often to one's lips. *Redemption* itself, that ancient and unchangeable redemption, that eternal joy of God's people, gives way to a more modern redemption that calls on the whole life of Jesus Christ without weighing itself down over his death and that pretends to absorb the sacrifice of the Son of man in the incarnation of the Son of God.[10]

---

[10] Meditate on John 12:27, Hebrews 2:14, etc. Far from subordinating redemption to the incarnation, this family of passages does the exact opposite. [A.M.]

It would be too difficult to accommodate Saint Paul to these innovations, but there is a theory right at hand to reassure a person as he is turning aside from the apostle's teachings. Saint Paul, it is said, had his own special mission amongst the apostles of Jesus Christ, just as Saint Peter and Saint James had theirs. Charged with setting forth the aspect of the gospel through which the Gentiles were to be won, Paul was able to and, indeed, had to clothe it in very neat, precise, and absolute terms that need to be tempered (not to say corrected) by Saint Peter's or Saint James' words, which are less systematic, less theological, and are, in any case, moving in a different direction.

IN DEFENSE OF GRACE

As for me, I would consider this objection to be adequately rebutted by what is written about the words of the prophets and is certainly no less true of the words of the apostles. "No prophecy was ever produced by the will of man, but men spoke from God as they were carried along by the Holy Spirit" (2 Peter 1:21). Yet to this first reason, which could only touch those who believe in the inspiration of the Scriptures, let us add considerations taken from the very nature of things.

First, Paul is the apostle to the Gentiles, which is to say he is our apostle. Consequently, if we had to choose among all the apostles, he is the one to whom we can listen with the most complete confidence, since he comes to us with a special message from God. Neither Peter nor James nor John himself have as much claim on us as Paul.

Then, being the apostle to the Gentiles—that is, to all the nations on earth but one—Paul was called by his very mission to present the gospel in its most general and yet most essential terms. If one were to fear some particularity, it would be with Peter or James, but the apostle to the Gentiles is the universal apostle, with whom one should seek only the common, permanent, substantive heart of the gospel.

Paul alone wrote more letters than all the other apostles put together, without counting the gospel of Saint Luke, which incontestably belongs to Paul's school. Very well, all things being equal, where will one more surely seek a complete exposition of saving truth: with Paul, treating in turn all the great questions of doctrine, morality, worship, and discipline, which he considers in their most varied aspects; or with Peter and James, whose teaching is concentrated in a few pages and confined to a relatively restrained circle?

Finally, Paul was born within Judaism and nourished within Pharisaism. Prejudice would thus draw him in a direction opposite to the doctrine of grace. This doctrine, far from revealing in him the characteristics of custom and training, has all those of a victory painfully won against inveterate tastes and deeply rooted habits. It might seem reasonable (I only say "seem") to suspect prejudice in James' and Peter's continuing tendency to lean in the direction in which they first fell.[11] There is no shadow of this with Paul, who has become a completely new man and is proclaiming a doctrine that he started out fiercely persecuting.

HOLDING FAST TO PAUL'S FAITH

No, no. Let us refrain from tolerating the least attack against the pure doctrine of the apostle Paul. Paul's faith is, after all, only the faith of Peter, John, and James, except for nuances of temperament and mission. Paul's faith is the faith

---

[11] That is, *if* one were to suspect prejudice it would not logically be on Paul's part but on that of the apostles to the Jews. Monod, as is clear below, is certainly not saying that there was or even seems to be prejudice in any of the apostolic writings. They were all preaching the same basic message.

of the apostolic century; it is the faith of the Reformation; it is the faith of our awakening; it is the faith of Jesus Christ; it is the intimate essence, the living marrow of the gospel. Is this not why the spirit of doubt or of half-faith chooses it as the preferred target for its attacks?

As for us, imitators of Paul, let us remain firm and unshakeable in this faith. Even as we grow in the truth, even as we eagerly greet whatever new light it pleases God to provide for us, let us also "show the same earnestness to have the full assurance of hope until the end" (Hebrews 6:11), the full assurance of that unique, that eternal hope, "Jesus Christ and him crucified" (1 Corinthians 2:2)! May we always be seen as so "rooted and grounded" (Ephesians 3:17) in the grace proclaimed by our holy apostle that our name could no more be separated from that grace than Paul's could!

IMITATING PAUL'S APOSTLESHIP

Imitating Saint Paul's Christianity would seem to be a career grand enough to tempt the highest Christian ambition. Yet, my brothers and sisters, in closing these discourses, I see an even grander career opening before us. If we follow the apostle in his Christian life through his Christian faith, we will not only be imitators of his Christianity, we will also be imitators of his apostleship. I said earlier that Paul was an apostle only through being a Christian, but in taking the path that I urge for you, and for me along with you, we too will be apostles through being Christians.[12]

---

[12] The term apostle is used differently in different Christian circles today. Here Monod is not talking about a mission comparable to the writing of the New Testament but one of spreading the gospel and witnessing to its truth through our lives. The Greek word for apostle literally means "one who is sent."

TASK OF OUR TIMES

Do not doubt that we too have our apostolic mission. It is not the mission of the first century; it is that of the nineteenth. It is not a question of carrying the gospel to the Gentiles; it is a question of rehabilitating it in the eyes of Christians. The gospel has been compromised in the religious awakening of our times because there hasn't been a visible difference between the lives of believers and those of non-believers that is proportional to the difference in their principles. Now it is a question of making the reality and power of faith visible to every eye.

The "salt has lost its taste; how shall its saltiness be restored?" (Matthew 5:13; Luke 14:34). This is the insoluble problem that it is time to resolve, and the solution, the true apostleship of our times, can only be given through the work of God's children today—or rather through the work of God's people today. This is not a job for one man, even if that man were a Saint Paul; this is a job for an entire population of brothers.

Someone might ask, "What would Saint Paul do if he were living today?" I don't know, but that is not the pressing question. The gospel remains the same; the means change. Perhaps, in God's plans, there isn't a task today prepared for a Saint Paul. However, there is one prepared for a population of Christians like Saint Paul, if you will allow me this expression, and this is the people that I am laboring to form or awaken through these discourses.

ALL TOGETHER

One could say that Paul himself enters into this thought. In my text, he doesn't simply write, "Imitate me;" he writes, "Join in imitating me," thereby urging a collective imitation. This is not to say that a lone Christian cannot do much for the cause of the practical apostleship I just mentioned. Like Saint Paul, he can prove through his example that the gospel requires nothing unfeasible, and this would remove the most formidable obstacle that truth encounters in upright hearts. But for this proof to become truly visible and decisive, it has to be offered not by some exceptional or isolated individual, but by an organic body where it shines simultaneously in each member and in the relationships between them.

I quite purposely said "an organic body," not "an organized body." I'm talking about the natural unity that arises spontaneously from a common life-principle, not about the manufactured uniformity produced through the choice of human will by a common administration. The people I am calling for is neither an association nor even a new church; it is a spiritual people, freely and yet necessarily united—united on the inside through the life of the spirit and on the outside through good works.

Saint Paul was calling for this before I was, in the lovely words that sum up all his discourses:

> For the grace of God has appeared, bringing salvation for all people, training us to renounce ungodliness and worldly passions, and to live self-controlled, upright, and godly lives in the present age, waiting for our blessed hope, the appearing of the glory of our great God and Savior Jesus Christ, who gave himself for us to redeem us from all lawlessness and to purify for himself a people for his own possession who are zealous for good works.[13] — Titus 2:11–14

You Christians, imitators of Saint Paul, the universal characteristic of the gospel is reality or, more to the point, it is incarnation. The Son of God, that living Word, had his

---

[13] Literally "*zealots* for good works," just as the Jews were "*zealots* for the law" (Acts 21:20, literal version). [A.M.]

incarnation in the Son of man. The revealed word must also have its own incarnation in a people of God in whom everyone can see what we preach put into practice and what we say lived out.

There, there is the contemporary religious work that is greater than that of the apostle Paul! There is the only work that holds the promise of spiritual renewal for Christianity! There is the unique hope of the spiritual, ecclesiastical, even political and social restoration that the world is sighing after on every side!

I am well aware that my voice is only a feeble though faithful echo of God's. Therefore may it be not my voice but the very voice of God that speaks today to the hearts of his children who are listening to me! And "on the day God leads his forces"—and is that day not coming?—may his people rise up as a "people who will offer themselves freely . . . in holy garments" and present "the dew of their youth" to him "from the womb of the morning" (see Psalm 110:3)! Amen.

OTHER TITLES FROM SOLID GROUND

In addition to Monod's *Saint Paul* and the other Monod Classics listed at the front of this edition, Solid Ground Christian Books has reprinted several volumes from the Puritan era, such as:

The Complete Works of Thomas Manton (in 22 volumes)
A Body of Divinity by Archbishop James Ussher
An Exposition of Hebrews by William Gouge
A Short Explanation of Hebrews by David Dickson
An Exposition of the Epistle of Jude by Thomas Jenkyn
A Commentary on the New Testament by John Trapp
Gospel Sonnets by Ralph Erskine
Heaven Upon Earth by James Janeway
The Marrow of True Justification by Benjamin Keach
The Travels of True Godliness by Benjamin Keach
The Redeemer's Tears Wept Over Lost Souls by John Howe
Commentary on the Second Epistle of Peter by Thomas Adams
The Christian Warfare by John Downame
An Exposition of the Ten Commandments by Ezekiel Hopkins
The Harmony of the Divine Attributes by William Bates
The Communicant's Companion by Matthew Henry
The Secret of Communion with God by Matthew Henry

View at www.solid-ground-books.com

Call us at 205-443-0311

CPSIA information can be obtained at www.ICGtesting.com
Printed in the USA
LVOW08s0901100716

495747LV00001B/18/P